CALIFORNIA

D1558880

DISASTERS

TRUE STORIES OF **GOLDEN STATE**
TRAGEDIES AND TRIUMPHS

PHYLLIS J. PERRY

FARCOUNTRY
PRESS

For David Perry, Barb Jernigan, and Will Harmon,
with gratitude for their help and encouragement in writing this book

ISBN: 978-1-56037-775-7

For more information about our books, write Farcountry Press,
P.O. Box 5630, Helena, MT 59604; call (800) 821-3874;
or visit www.farcountrypress.com.

Produced and printed in the United States of America.

25 24 23 22   1 2 3 4 5 6

CONTENTS

ACKNOWLEDGMENTS

SPECIAL THANKS GO TO BARB JERNIGAN FOR ENCOURAGEMENT AND assistance with sources, and to Claudia Mills, who cheered me along this journey through *California Disasters.* Also to my editor, Will Harmon, for his dedication to every aspect of this project.

EDITOR'S NOTE

AS PRODUCTION ON THIS BOOK WAS WRAPPING UP IN 2021, WILDFIRES continued to burn in parts of California. Unfortunately, those stories of loss and heroism could not be included here; indeed, the stories of the state's wildfires could fill another volume of equal size. Yet one dramatic scene from the 2021 fire season is worth mentioning. On September 9, lightning sparked the KNP Complex Fire in Sequoia National Park, and flames advanced toward groves of giant sequoias, including the world's largest tree, the General Sherman. The images of fire crews clearing brush and wrapping fire-resistant foil around the base of this great tree are now an indelible part of history. One of those photos is featured on the back cover of this book to capture the ongoing story of how people work to overcome and recover from disaster.

INTRODUCTION

A Disaster for Every Season

THERE'S AN OLD SAYING THAT CALIFORNIA HAS FOUR SEASONS: earthquake, fire, flood, and drought. This may be a little harsh on the sunny state of California, but it's an apt summary of the many disasters that have occurred in the Golden State over the past 200 years.

What is a disaster? A disaster is an event that causes either loss of life, extensive property damage, or both. Disasters can be caused by humans or by various forces of nature. They can affect a single person or many people, and they can take many different forms. Every state in the nation has experienced any number of remarkable disasters. California has suffered thousands of them, some of them dating back to before statehood.

This book isn't an attempt to document all or even most California disasters. Rather, it recounts a few of the most dramatic and diverse ones—and at least one that was a near miss. Within these pages are stories of a volcanic eruption in which no lives were lost but also earthquakes and fires where thousands died. Here, too, are stories of floods and droughts; disasters involving ships, planes, trains, and cars; shark attacks; mine fires; and avalanches. Some of these disasters occurred long ago, while others were very recent.

Survivors of disasters experience loss, but they also may gain hard-won knowledge. The stories in this book help to share not only tragic experiences but also, perhaps, some of the knowledge. It never hurts to be prepared. After all, disasters will continue to occur. A new one may be happening somewhere even as you read this book. To learn more about preparing for, responding to, and mitigating disasters where you live, visit www.ready. gov, a national public-service website designed to educate and empower Americans faced by emergencies, including natural and man-made disasters.

BIG EARTHQUAKES

EARTHQUAKES ARE A WELL-KNOWN HAZARD OF LIFE IN CALIFORNIA. An average of 258 quakes of magnitude 3.0 or greater strike the state each year, a rate second only to Alaska. One or two of those is usually strong enough to cause damage. Since 1850, the state has seen 72 "big" quakes of 6.0 magnitude or greater, an average of one about every two years. Why are earthquakes so frequent in California?

The answer lies deep underground, where the Pacific tectonic plate meets and subsides beneath the North American plate. The boundary between these two chunks of the Earth's crust happens to run along California's coast from Cape Mendocino to the Mexican border near Mexicali. Numerous other faults slice across California's landscape. Here are the stories from a few of the more interesting big quakes in California's history.

THE EARTHQUAKES OF DECEMBER 1812

Beginning in 1769, Spain built a string of twenty-one missions in its North American territory of *Alta California* (Spanish for Upper California). They stretched for 650 miles near the coastline. Each was about 30 miles from the next, making it a long day's horseback ride between them. The first and southernmost was Mission San Diego. The last and northernmost was Mission San Francisco Solano, dedicated in 1824. It was located in what is present-day Sonoma. It was the only mission built in *Alta California* after Mexico gained independence from Spain in 1821. Although there were only about 400 Native Americans at this mission, an estimated 32,000 Indians worshipped at missions throughout the system during the early 1800s.

In addition to the missions, the Spaniards also built presidios—military garrisons or forts. The purpose of the missions was to establish claim to this land for Spain. The Native Americans of the region would be taught Spanish, become Catholics, learn more about agriculture, and in time establish small Spanish towns. The presidios would protect those at the missions from hostile natives, and, if needed, from incursions by other European powers such as Russia.

Mission San Juan Capistrano was one of nine missions founded by Father Junípero Serra, a Franciscan priest who became known as the Apostle of California for his missionary work among the natives there. The old adobe church in this area was too small, and a new, larger stone church was completed in 1806. San Juan Capistrano was the seventh of the string of twenty-one *Alta California* missions.

It wasn't easy for indigenous people to adapt to life in the missions. The Spanish introduced horses, mules, oxen, cattle, and sheep. They brought a new language, foods, clothing, and ideas. The Spanish also unintentionally introduced diseases to which the Native Americans had no immunity. An estimated 65,000 Native Americans lived in this mission coastal region in 1770, but by 1839 their numbers had fallen to 17,000.

SAN JUAN CAPISTRANO EARTHQUAKE

Early on the morning of December 8, 1812, in the great stone church at Mission San Juan Capistrano, forty devout Native American worshippers were gathered for morning mass. Suddenly the ground began to shake

This sketch from 1916 by Rexford Newcomb depicts the original stone church
at Mission San Juan Capistrano, complete with bell tower.
IMAGE IN THE PUBLIC DOMAIN.

violently. Heavy beams and rock walls came crashing down, killing all of them. The death toll would likely have been higher if disease had not already decimated the local population.

Immediately after the earthquake, the missionaries did not try to rebuild the church. Instead, they worshipped in their old, small church. After a Mexican governor arrived in 1824, the native people were advised that they no longer had to obey the commands of the Franciscans. San Juan Capistrano was chosen as the site for a pueblo of free Indians in 1833, and mission activities ceased. The adjacent land soon became the property of white settlers.

In 1845, the mission was sold to Don Juan Forster, whose family lived there for twenty years. President Abraham Lincoln returned the mission to the Catholic Church in 1865. Father John O'Sullivan came to the mission in 1910 and began restoring the church that stands on the grounds today. Visitors can still see the ruins of the old stone church. A new parish church built in the style of the old one stands nearby.

The ruins of the old stone church at Mission San Juan Capistrano still stand today.
PHOTOGRAPH BY BERNARD GAGNON, CC BY-SA 3.0.

This California earthquake of 1812 is sometimes called the San Juan Capistrano Earthquake because of the death toll at the mission, but it's also referred to as the Wrightwood Earthquake. Accurate records from that time are simply not available, but based on written accounts and evidence from such things as sediments and tree rings, some scientists think that the earthquake happened along the Mojave segment of the San Andreas Fault. The ground surface was likely ruptured for as much as 106 miles, with the epicenter located near today's community of Wrightwood, 77 miles northeast of Los Angeles. Researchers estimate the quake to have been between a magnitude of 6.0 and 7.5 on the Richter scale. Damage from the earthquake was also reported at the missions of San Gabriel and San Diego.

New scientific data reported by Julian Lozoz, an assistant professor of geophysics at California State University-Northridge, suggests that the quake started along the San Jacinto Fault and caused the nearby San Andreas Fault to rupture as well.

LA PURISIMA EARTHQUAKE

A second damaging quake struck *Alta California* two weeks later on December 21, 1812. At Mission La Purisima in Lompoc Valley, at about 10 A.M., the earth began to shake. The residents of the mission, which included Native Americans, padres, and soldiers, became frightened and ran outside. The people were huddled together talking when, fifteen minutes later, a second shock came. This one was stronger, and the shaking caused the mission bells to begin ringing. The adobe walls of the mission cracked and some portions collapsed. A few people were injured, but no one was crushed and killed by falling debris.

The missionaries reported that a crack in the ground appeared in a hill south of the mission and that, three days after the earthquake, the mission site was covered with mud that washed out of the crack. The damage was so severe that the mission was abandoned. A new Mission La Purisima was built several miles north of the original site.

This earthquake not only left Mission La Purisima in shambles, it completely destroyed Mission Santa Barbara. There was also damage to the Santa Barbara Presidio, Mission Santa Buenaventura, Mission Santa Ines, and Mission San Fernando, covering a distance of over 100 miles.

At Santa Barbara, rather than return to the presidio, the soldiers built thatched huts where they lived while aftershocks from the quake continued. It was March, almost three months after the initial quake, before the soldiers dared to enter the presidio again. A seismic sea wave associated with the

Only ruins of Mission La Purisima remained standing in 1904 when this image was taken.
PHOTOGRAPH BY CHARLES C. PIERCE, COURTESY OF THE CALIFORNIA HISTORICAL SOCIETY.

earthquake is credited with damaging a Spanish ship that was at anchor twenty-eight miles offshore. There are also reports, believed by some but disputed by others, that this earthquake spawned a tsunami at Refugio Canyon near the northwestern end of the Santa Barbara Channel. It was said to have caused the abandonment of the Chumash villages on Santa Rosa Island.

The epicenter of this second quake is also uncertain. It might have been inland in what is now Santa Barbara, or it could have been offshore in the Santa Barbara Channel. The magnitude was estimated at 7.0 No deaths were reported from the December 21 earthquake.

From these two examples, it would be easy to infer that it is safer to run outside a building when a quake strikes, but decades of data suggest otherwise. Research shows that most injuries happen when people try to leave a building during the quake. Experts say the best reaction is to drop, cover, and hold on. Get under a table or desk, hold onto it, and stay there until the shaking stops. If no table or desk is available, tuck into an inside corner where two structural walls meet and cover your head with your arms. Visit the California Earthquake Authority website for more information on earthquake preparedness.

SAN FRANCISCO EARTHQUAKE AND FIRE, 1906

Awakened from a sound sleep early in the morning by the violent shaking of his bed, sixteen-year-old Sol Lesser was suddenly thrown to the floor as doors came unhinged and pictures dangled from walls in the house. Through the open window came the sounds of splintering glass and chimneys crashing into the street below. Outside, Sol heard the voices of people in their nightclothes, confused and too afraid to go back inside their houses. Such were the recollections of Sol regarding the Wednesday morning of the April 18, 1906, San Francisco Earthquake. Thousands of people told similar tales. Some were much more terrifying.

The first sign of trouble was a strong foreshock at 5:12 A.M. About twenty seconds later, the main quake struck. The quake was so strong it was felt from the southern border of Oregon to south of Los Angeles and as far inland as the middle of Nevada. With a magnitude of between 7.7 and 8.3 on the Richter scale, the quake ruptured 296 miles of the San Andreas Fault from San Juan Batista to Cape Mendocino.

The San Andreas Fault is a fissure in the Earth's crust that extends more than 600 miles. It runs along the boundary between the North American tectonic plate to the east and the Pacific plate to the west. The Pacific plate is moving south, while the North American plate is moving north at about two inches a year. But these plates don't just creep along. Sometimes they stick, and tremendous stress builds until the plates suddenly shift—an earthquake occurs.

The epicenter of the 1906 earthquake was in the ocean about two miles west of San Francisco. But modern-day researchers have found that the shaking was centered on two points: near Point Reyes to the north and on the San Francisco Peninsula to the south.

At this time, San Francisco was the largest city in California, with a population of about 400,000 people. The business district held some skyscrapers, and most buildings were constructed of wood and bricks. Around the bay, many buildings rested on landfill—soil, rock, and debris deposited in the water to build up and extend the shoreline. This "made land" liquefied as it shook during the quake and took on the consistency of quicksand. As their foundations sank, many buildings on the landfill collapsed. The four-story Valencia Hotel, south of Market Street, was one such building. It shuddered and crashed in on itself as the first three floors sank into the liquified ground. Only the fourth floor remained above ground. As many as 200 people were trapped in the hotel, many of whom drowned as broken water mains flooded the sunken building. Buildings constructed on bedrock fared slightly better, although construction standards of the day were insufficient in the face of such a powerful quake. Brick facades and chimneys tumbled into the streets, walls collapsed, and

The Valencia Hotel sank and crumbled when the quake liquified the ground it was built on.
PHOTOGRAPH BY BEAR PHOTO, COURTESY OF THE U.S. GEOLOGICAL SURVEY.

foundations slanted at crazy angles. Fissures appeared, and in places the streets rose and fell and rose again, displacing pavement and trolley lines.

San Francisco had suffered earthquakes before—including in 1853, 1868, 1898, and 1900—but none of them compared to this. The vigorous shaking lasted about forty-five to sixty seconds and was followed by many strong aftershocks. Destruction from the quake itself was severe, but even worse was yet to come as fires broke out all over the city. The fires swept from the business section of town to Russian Hill, Chinatown, North Beach, and Telegraph Hill. The initial earthquake tremors ruptured the city's gas and water mains. The fire department was almost helpless without streams of water to fight the flames. Also, many streets were clogged with debris, making travel almost impossible. One of the first casualties was Fire Chief Engineer Dennis T. Sullivan, who was killed when a chimney from the California Theater fell into the fire station where he was living.

Within an hour of the earthquake, the San Francisco Fire Department had requested soldiers to help contain the fire. Within a few hours, an artillery division from Fort Miley came to help. U.S. Navy personnel also went into action. Using a destroyer and two tugboats, sailors pumped seawater from the bay to fight the fire along the waterfront. Their efforts saved a number of gold rush–era buildings.

City Hall collapsed, so the Hall of Justice became the command center. Officials devised a desperate plan to use dynamite to create a fire break and stop the forward path of the fire, but this was dangerous and counterintuitive. No one wanted to blow up a building that wasn't already burning, and yet by waiting for a building to catch fire before acting, it made the task even more difficult and dangerous. Firefighters untrained in handling dynamite had to carry the explosive into areas where buildings were burning and sparks flying. Unfortunately, the rubble of some dynamited buildings caught fire anyway. Winds blew the flames in various directions; battling the fire on a single front was impossible.

Jails also were threatened by the quake and fires. Prisoners feared walls would collapse on them or they would be left to face death by fire. It was finally decided to evacuate the jails, and police and National Guardsmen marched the prisoners to a wharf and got them aboard a ship. They were eventually taken to Alcatraz Island, where about 200 prisoners were housed for a couple of weeks before being moved to other jails. The prison on Alcatraz, built directly on rock, suffered little damage during the earthquake.

Heroic and desperate measures were taken, but with so much of the city on fire, it seemed nothing could stop the flames. The fires eventually consumed five square miles—500 city blocks—of office buildings and

People watch flames engulf San Francisco after the 1906 earthquake.
PHOTOGRAPH COURTESY OF THE P. E. HOTZ COLLECTION, U.S. GEOLOGICAL SURVEY.

homes. More than 250,000 San Francisco residents were left homeless.

The presence of soldiers in the city led some to think that martial law had been declared, but this wasn't the case. Soldiers did patrol the city, discouraging looters and directing clean-up efforts. In addition to police, Marines, and Navy personnel, members of the California National Guard (which the governor had mobilized) and a so-called citizen's guard (a vigilante group deputized by the mayor) patrolled the streets to prevent looting and mayhem. These various groups were not well coordinated, and there were many jurisdictional disputes. As a result of all the confusion, a few innocent bystanders were shot and killed.

Telephone and telegraph lines were down, and the city was isolated. It was hard to get accurate information about what was happening. Within hours of the earthquake, the local *Daily News* printed a one-sheet edition that included a list of the known dead and injured. Without electrical power at the paper's Mission Street printing plant, printers used a hand-cranked press, running new editions until they were forced to leave as fires neared the building.

Not knowing where to go or what to do, residents remained outside, milling in the streets. Thousands of people gathered in Lafayette Square. A wagonload of food arrived and was quickly distributed. Many residents, fearing further quakes and terrified by the fires, rushed to leave the city. A few went to Fisherman's Wharf and boarded boats headed north to Sausalito. Most struggled through crowded streets to the Ferry Building, hoping to make their way to the East Bay. Mark Lewis Gerstle wrote in his memoir:

> The fire was eventually stopped at Van Ness Avenue by marines from the navy yard, who dynamited all the buildings on the east side of Van Ness so that the fire did not cross the Avenue at that point, although it did get across lower Van Ness Avenue. The Sloss house on the corner of Van Ness and Pine, and the Lilienthal houses adjoining, were all dynamited with all their valuables.

One of the terrified people in San Francisco during the earthquake was the world-famous tenor Enrico Caruso. He had performed the night before the quake with the traveling New York Metropolitan Opera Company in San Francisco's opera house (the dome of which collapsed the next morning during the earthquake). He was staying that night at the seven-story Palace Hotel. It was the largest and most luxurious hotel on the West Coast, with 755 rooms and large hydraulic elevators called "rising rooms" paneled in redwood. Caruso wrote an account that was printed in London in *The Sketch*, containing his observations that morning:

> I wake up at about 5 o'clock, feeling my bed rocking as though I am on a ship in the ocean. . . . I get up and go to the window, raise the shade and look out. And what I see makes me tremble with fear. I see the buildings toppling, big pieces of masonry falling, and from the street below I hear the cries and screams of men, and women, and children.

Caruso and all the guests at the Palace Hotel were lucky. They escaped unharmed. In fact, Caruso's valet returned, packed all of the tenor's belongings, dragged the trunks one at a time down six flights of stairs, secured a cab, and got the singer and all his belongings to the Ferry Building, where Caruso escaped from the city and took a train back to New York. He vowed never to return to San Francisco—a promise that he kept.

Author Jack London and his wife, Charmian, lived forty miles north of San Francisco. They were awakened by the earthquake and claimed they could see smoke from the San Francisco fires in the distance. London received a telegram from *Collier's* magazine asking him to write an article about the earthquake for them. London accepted the assignment, and he and Charmian headed toward the city, watching the great fires first from a boat in the bay and then on foot in the city itself. London's article appeared the following month, illustrated with many of his own photos taken on glass plate negatives. He wrote of walking through the city center, much of which at that time was still standing as the fires approached. He described watching the fire move in and destroy Union Square. He wrote of people wandering the streets wrapped in blankets and carrying bundles of belongings. Some families pulled wagons full of their possessions. Baby buggies, wagons, and anything with wheels were used to carry goods, and many people were simply dragging trunks behind them. In spite of all this, London commented on the courtesy shown by people to one another. Soldiers kept the crowds moving, although in some cases exhausted people gave up and abandoned their trunks, leaving them to be consumed by the approaching fire. Fires continued on Thursday and into Friday, sweeping through Russian Hill and Telegraph Hill, and destroying most of the city's wharves and docks.

Some San Franciscans took refuge in neighboring communities. These refugees were fed through government and private relief efforts. On April 20, with most of the fires out, San Francisco Mayor Eugene Schmitz appointed two large committees to supervise relief work and reconstruction efforts. The relief committee had many subcommittees, including Relief of the Hungry, Housing the Homeless, and Restoration of Water. Activities to keep people safe and healthy were organized, such as baking and distributing

As fires consumed the city, many San Franciscans fled,
lugging whatever belongings they could manage.
PHOTOGRAPH COURTESY OF THE U.S. GEOLOGICAL SURVEY.

bread, supplying clothing, collecting garbage, and boiling drinking water. But many people simply wanted to leave the city. The Southern Pacific Railroad offered free transportation to any Bay Area citizens who wanted to travel out of the state, and 100,000 people took advantage.

Most of the large banks in San Francisco burned in the fires that swept the city. Their vaults, containing currency, gold, and important papers, remained closed for weeks afterward for fear that any paper in the vaults might catch fire when oxygen rushed in. But one small bank in the Italian neighborhood of North Beach, named the Bank of Italy, seized the opportunity presented by the disaster. The bank was founded and managed by Amadeo P. Giannini, the son of Italian immigrants, who initially had made his living by selling fruits and vegetables from a wagon. When flames threatened his one-room bank, Giannini took $80,000 in gold coins from the bank vault. He hid the coins under crates of oranges and safely passed looters in the streets. In the days that followed, he set up a makeshift bank on the wharf in North Beach and gave loans on a handshake. Gradually, by traveling across the state and by inspiring confidence and encouraging working-class people, especially farmers, to use his bank, he opened

The devastation to a once-thriving city was stunning.
PHOTOGRAPH BY G. R. DAVIS, COURTESY OF THE U.S. GEOLOGICAL SURVEY.

the nation's first system of statewide branches. In 1930, the Bank of Italy changed its name to Bank of America. By 1949, it was the largest bank in the world, with more than 500 branches. Out of this massive disaster, a large and successful business was born.

For a significant number of Chinese people, another positive came out of the devastating earthquake and fire. Many of the residents of Chinatown weren't citizens. A person born in the United States was automatically a citizen, but the laws at that time made it almost impossible for others to obtain citizenship. The 1900 census listed 11,000 Chinese living in San Francisco, but the actual number was probably closer to 25,000. Since the fire destroyed so many buildings, countless records were burned. As a result, some residents of Chinatown simply claimed that they were citizens and that their birth certificates had burned. With no records to contradict their claims, they obtained the rights of citizenship.

Many hoped other positives would come out of the disaster. With the city of San Francisco in ruins, some saw opportunities to rebuild a better-planned and safer city. Insurance companies set up tents to conduct business and handle losses, and restoration began immediately; some people simply wanted to rebuild as quickly as possible, ignoring any lessons they might have learned about earthquake safety and better building methods and materials.

Remarkably, within two years, little trace of the earthquake and fires remained. In fact, ready to show the world how quickly it had recovered, San Francisco hosted the Panama-Pacific International Exposition in 1915 to celebrate the completion of the Panama Canal. The fairgrounds were constructed on a 636-acre site on the northern shore, between the Presidio and Fort Mason, an area now called the Marina District.

In all, the death toll from the earthquake and fires was estimated at more than 3,000 in San Francisco and 189 elsewhere, including in Santa Rosa and San Jose. More than 28,000 buildings were destroyed. The San Andreas Fault remains active, generating numerous relatively small earthquakes every year.

THE WORLD SERIES EARTHQUAKE, 1989

In the history of Major League Baseball's World Series, championship matchups between teams from the same state aren't unheard of, but neither are they common. They typically generate more than the usual amount of excitement among devotees of the sport, especially when the teams aren't just from the same state but from neighboring metropolises. Such rivalries bring extra intensity to the field of play, and this was the case in October 1989 when the Oakland Athletics and San Francisco Giants faced off for a best-of-seven-game World Series billed as the Battle of the Bay. Prior to Game 3, however, no one knew just how intense game day would become.

The Athletics, known as the A's, had won the first two games of the series at their home field in Oakland. For the third game on October 17, the teams were scheduled to meet at Candlestick Park on the bay south of downtown San Francisco. As more than 60,000 excited fans found their seats and watched the pre-game festivities, hundreds of thousands more tuned in on their televisions. ABC sportscasters Tim McCarver and Al Michaels went live at 5 P.M., recapping highlights from the previous game.

Suddenly, at 5:04 P.M., the video signal on all those television screens broke up. McCarver stumbled over his words as the stadium began to shake violently. Viewers heard Al Michaels say, "I'll tell you what, we're having an earth—" and then the feed went dead.

The epicenter of this earthquake, which proved to be a magnitude 6.9, was near Loma Prieta Peak in the Santa Cruz Mountains, about sixty miles southeast of San Francisco and Candlestick Park. It originated on a fault adjacent to the San Andreas Fault system, about nine miles northeast of Santa Cruz. The San Andreas system is part of the boundary between the Pacific and North American tectonic plates. In this case, the plates abruptly slipped about seven feet.

Though the quake struck without warning, scientists wondered later if there hadn't been signs that a big one was coming. In June 1988 and again in August 1989, a pair of magnitude 5.0 earthquakes had rattled the Lake Elsman area not far from the October quake's epicenter. Seismologists believed that these were foreshocks to the Loma Prieta quake. After each of these events, the state Office of Emergency Services issued an advisory that there was a higher than usual risk of a large earthquake in the area. The 5.3-magnitude quake in June 1988 caused broken windows in Los Gatos and some minor damage in Holy City. The 5.4-magnitude quake in August1989 toppled chimneys in Los Gatos and Cupertino, and one person was killed.

When the temblor hit on October 17, freeways and bridges in the area were less crowded than usual because so many people were at the World Series game or home watching it on television. This probably kept the death toll lower than it might have been. All told, the Loma Prieta Earthquake (also known as the World Series Earthquake) caused 67 deaths, 3,757 injuries, and an estimated $6.8 billion in damage.

The largest cluster of fatalities occurred in Oakland when the Cypress Street Viaduct on the Nimitz Freeway collapsed. This freeway had two

The upper level of the Cypress Street Viaduct collapsed
onto the lower deck, buckling support pillars.
PHOTOGRAPH BY G. PLAFKER, U.S. GEOLOGICAL SURVEY.

raised levels. When the upper level fell, it crushed cars beneath it and led to crashes on the upper level. Many of the vehicles caught fire, and smoke from the burning cars and dust from the collapse of the freeway filled the sky. Residents of the area rushed to help victims, at great risk to themselves, even as aftershocks shook the damaged roadway. These rescuers were already on the scene when two companies of the Oakland Fire Department arrived.

Rescuers climbed onto the upper deck and ran from car to car searching for survivors. Many wore kerchiefs over their noses and mouths because of the smoke and dust. The neighbors on the scene worked with police and firefighters to raise ladders and carry victims to safety. Some survivors were able to walk away from their cars. Others were injured or trapped in burning cars. Some were trapped under sections of vehicles or chunks of concrete. The survivors who could walk used a telescoping ladder to climb down to receive first-aid.

In one case, a recreational vehicle smashed into a semi-truck, trapping the driver under the RV dashboard. It took firefighters forty-five minutes to cut him out. He was placed on a stretcher, carried down the ladder, and taken away for medical attention.

Freeing and helping victims went on all night. Four days later, an inspecting engineer found a victim still alive in his vehicle, spared from being crushed by a large beam that fell across the car. The man had a fractured skull and broken ribs. He received get-well cards from all over the world before he succumbed to his injuries and died a month later. All told, forty-two people died in the Nimitz Freeway collapse.

Eighteen of Oakland's twenty-one fire companies worked on the rescue and were assisted by all branches of the military as well as fire companies from as far away as Los Angeles. Departments in some neighboring cities were unable to send help because they were busy with their own earthquake emergencies. Three days after the event, President George H. W. Bush came to Santa Cruz to view the damage. He signed a $1.1 billion relief package for the state.

A fifty-foot section of the San Francisco–Oakland Bay Bridge also collapsed, claiming yet another life. Rescuers managed to pull a car that was dangling over the edge of the bridge back up onto the roadway, but two occupants—a man and a woman—were seriously injured. A Coast Guard helicopter landed on the bridge and took the casualties to the Letterman Army Medical Center Hospital, the only facility nearby with a helipad. The woman was dead on arrival, while her brother eventually recovered.

Candlestick Park held up well during the World Series Earthquake. There was a long crack in section 53, and a few chunks of concrete fell. No in-

One person died when a section of the Bay Bridge collapsed.
PHOTOGRAPH COURTESY OF THE U.S. GEOLOGICAL SURVEY.

juries were reported. Officials postponed the game, and the huge crowd filed out and got into their cars, wondering which roads remained open to carry them home.

San Francisco's Marina District suffered considerable damage from the quake. Many of the buildings there were built on fill, including rubble dumped into the bay after the 1906 San Francisco Earthquake. The shaking caused liquefaction of this fill, which led to the partial or complete collapse of about seventy buildings. Many gas mains and pipes burst, sparking fires in the area. Soldiers from the Presidio Fire Station were called in to help,

Rescuers search for victims in the wreckage of the Pacific Garden Mall in Santa Cruz.
PHOTOGRAPH COURTESY OF THE U.S. GEOLOGICAL SURVEY.

but they reported that local fire hydrants stopped supplying water to their trucks after about twenty minutes due to aftershocks.

Nearer the epicenter, Santa Cruz County suffered heavy damage, as did Monterey and Los Gatos. There were numerous landslides in the Santa Cruz Mountains, and a tsunami (which caused no damage) was observed in Monterey Bay about ten minutes after the main shock.

The commercial district of Santa Cruz lost more than three dozen buildings, including clothing stores, a café, a department store, bookstores, and a hotel. A woman was killed in the department store, and two young workers died when a wall fell on them in the Santa Cruz Coffee Roasting Company.

Another hard-hit area was Watsonville, about seven miles from the epicenter. One in eight houses in the town were destroyed, along with 30 percent of the downtown. That night, people who had lost homes or were afraid to enter still-standing homes slept in cars or tents.

Although the quake lasted fifteen to forty seconds in San Francisco, the shaking continued in the Santa Cruz Mountains for up to six minutes.

There were ninety aftershocks of a magnitude greater than 3.0, with one measuring 5.2. In Santa Cruz County, about 5,000 chimneys fell, and the estimate of damage countywide was $84.9 million. Thousands were left homeless in Santa Cruz and Watsonville. Sixty to eighty percent of the roads in the area required repair, and California Highway 17 was closed to regular traffic for thirty-three days.

As bad as the World Series Earthquake was, some national media reports made it sound even more dire. While local reports tended to be accurate, national reports were not; they greatly exaggerated the number of deaths and the extent of the damage and reported that airport runways were damaged and flights were canceled, which was not the case. They also neglected to comment on the damage in Santa Cruz and Watsonville.

The World Series Earthquake left a legacy of challenges to be addressed in the days, weeks, months, and even years that followed. The broken piece of the San Francisco–Oakland Bay Bridge was restored and reopened in a month. Repairs to streets and roads continued for months. When the viaduct of the Nimitz Freeway, where the greatest loss of life occurred, was replaced, it was built as a single- rather than a double-deck structure. The freeway was not reopened until 1997.

At least 411 lawsuits were filed as a result of the quake, and two years later many were still pending. In San Francisco, 240 buildings were tagged as unsafe for human occupancy. Some businesses in Santa Cruz continued operating from tents for the next three years. Engineers determined that Candlestick Park had suffered only cosmetic damage, so Games 3 and 4 of the World Series were played there on October 27 and 28. The Athletics won both games, sweeping the series.

NORTHRIDGE EARTHQUAKE, 1994

In a 2014 *Los Angeles Times* retrospective reflecting back twenty years, Tom Mills recounted his experience on the night of the Northridge Earthquake. He and his wife had just moved to Los Angeles from New York the week before. They were spending their second night in their new apartment, looking forward to delivery of their furniture the next morning. Without a bed, they were sleeping on the floor. When the great shaking began, Tom and his wife huddled together in the empty living room, not knowing if this was a waking nightmare or reality. Holding a flashlight, Tom shakily asked, "Is this what they mean by an earthquake in L.A.?" The next day, Mills and his wife realized the enormity of the disaster as they drove through blocks of damaged and destroyed homes along Wilshire Boulevard in Santa Monica. They would never forget this unsettling welcome to California.

At 4:31 A.M. on January 17, 1994, the 6.7-magnitude Northridge Earthquake struck the San Fernando Valley in Southern California about twenty miles northwest of downtown Los Angeles. The epicenter was nine miles beneath the town of Reseda. Hardest hit was a thirty-mile circle around the Northridge neighborhood of Los Angeles, although the shaking was felt as far away as Las Vegas, Nevada. Only a minute after the initial quake, an aftershock with a magnitude of 6.0 struck the same area. Another 6.0 aftershock followed about eleven hours later, and many smaller aftershocks were recorded. A previously unknown thrust fault had ruptured, making the ground shift as much as ten feet at once. Much of the force of the quake went toward the mountains that line the northern side of the valley. For ten to twenty seconds, the ground shook both horizontally and vertically.

Los Angeles Mayor Richard Riordan and California Governor Pete Wilson both quickly declared a state of emergency. Wilson called out the National Guard, and President Bill Clinton issued a federal disaster declaration. Fire-rescue teams from throughout the state, even as far away as San Francisco, responded to the disaster in Los Angeles.

Including heart attacks attributed to the stress of the quake, the death toll reached 72, with another 12,000 people injured, 1,600 of them requiring hospitalization. Monetarily, it was the costliest earthquake in U.S. history, with an estimated $20 billion in property losses and another $29 billion in lost economic activity. The California Office of Emergency Services later reported that more than 681,000 residents and businesses—a state record—applied for federal disaster aid.

The largest cluster of deaths occurred at Northridge Meadows, a 163-unit apartment complex. The entire three-story building collapsed, crushing apartments on the first floor and killing sixteen people who lived in them. Among the occupants of the building was Mike Kubeisy, who set to work saving lives immediately after he was shaken awake. He rescued people from the rubble and managed to coax one frightened young woman named Patricia Silden to safety, guiding her step by step down a rickety ladder. Kubeisy is credited with saving five lives, including that of a Los Angeles police officer who also lived in the apartment complex. "I felt great that I was able to help," Kubeisy said, "but I wonder how I would've felt if I had turned my back on them. That's the thing I don't want to live with." Later that year, Kubeisy and Silden married and eventually had two sons. Kubeisy went on to a distinguished photography career in Hollywood, shooting stills for hit television shows such as *NCIS*, *House*, and *Grey's Anatomy*.

Many Northridge apartment complexes did not withstand the 6.7-magnitude 1994 quake.
PHOTOGRAPH COURTESY OF THE FEDERAL EMERGENCY MANAGEMENT AGENCY.

Because the tremor struck a densely developed region, damage to infrastructure was widespread and severe. The quake toppled buildings, freeways, and utility poles. The Earthquake Country Alliance, a statewide grassroots partnership that promotes earthquake preparedness, estimated that 82,000 residential and commercial properties were damaged. Also damaged or destroyed were 5,400 mobile homes and nine multilevel parking garages. Although the worst damage was sustained in the western and northern sections of the valley, other parts of Los Angeles County suffered damage, too, including the cities of Santa Monica, Santa Clarita, and Simi Valley. After the quake, tens of thousands of homes were red-tagged, which meant they were unsafe to enter. Thousands of others were yellow-tagged, limiting the number of occupants who could enter the building.

As a result of the earthquake, 20,000 people were displaced. Some became homeless because their apartment or home had been destroyed or badly damaged. Others lived in cars or camped out in parks, afraid to be indoors in case there were more aftershocks. Still others fled from snapped gas lines and water mains and from fires that broke out all over the area. By one count, the quake caused 110 fires. At Sylmar, seventy homes were

Throughout Northridge, broken gas mains led to fires
in buildings and within ruptured roadways.
PHOTOGRAPH COURTESY OF THE U.S. GEOLOGICAL SURVEY.

destroyed by fires started from gas leaks. In other places, severed underground gas lines and water mains resulted in some streets experiencing both fires and floods. Five days after the earthquake, about 50,000 customers were still without water service.

Across the Los Angeles area, many businesses, museums, and event venues were forced to close. Several shopping malls had major damage. In the Northridge Fashion Mall, where the Bullock's Department Store partially collapsed, no one was caught in the rubble, but hundreds of animals from a pet store needed help. In Santa Monica, there was significant property damage, especially to apartment buildings. In Valencia, the California Institute of the Arts was forced to close and relocate its classes to other facilities for the remainder of the year. The University of Southern California saw damage to older buildings, three of which were deemed irreparable and later razed. In Anaheim, the scoreboard in Anaheim Stadium collapsed onto hundreds of seats below, and several commercial buildings collapsed.

All aspects of transportation and communication were affected. Power and telephone services were out. The Los Angeles airport closed briefly. Rail service, both Amtrak and Metrolink, was interrupted for several days. Rail passengers instead rode buses to make their connections to travel beyond the city. A sixty-four-car Southern Pacific freight train carrying hazardous material derailed between Chatsworth and Northridge. One of sixteen tanker cars spewed a cloud of sulfuric acid, and the locomotive spilled 2,000 gallons of diesel fuel.

The Los Angeles metropolitan area is crossed by a network of freeways that serves millions of people, and these suffered tremendous damage. Five freeways were immediately closed, bringing traffic to a standstill. Sections of the Golden State Freeway had collapsed. At the Newhall Pass Interchange, a motorcycle officer with the Los Angeles Police Department, riding southbound in the morning darkness, failed to see that the roadway before him had collapsed and fell forty feet to his death. Many bridges were down. The Santa Monica Freeway, one of the busiest freeways in the United States, was in ruins. Rerouting traffic while repairs were made disrupted commutes for three months after the event. The Antelope Valley Freeway collapsed just as it had twenty-three years earlier during the Sylmar Earthquake, despite subsequent structural improvements.

Damage to infrastructure, including freeways, was extensive.
PHOTOGRAPH COURTESY OF THE U.S. GEOLOGICAL SURVEY.

Eleven hospitals were damaged, and nine were evacuated. This put a severe strain on undamaged hospitals that had to take in transferred patients as well as new casualties from the earthquake. One couple had a particularly harrowing experience. Tom and Peggy O'Donohue were awake when the quake hit. Peggy, pregnant and eight days overdue, was having contractions. As soon as the ground stopped shaking, they left their damaged home and drove through a chaotic scene of fires and destroyed buildings to a hospital. They sought safety from the aftershocks but were told the hospital was being evacuated. So they drove to Northridge Hospital. No beds were available, but a doctor found a gurney for Peggy and delivered her son. Shortly thereafter, the O'Donohues were told to vacate the room to make way for earthquake victims. Tom drove Peggy and their infant to Peggy's parents' home, where they sat in chairs in the driveway, afraid to risk going inside a house that might collapse. Their son, named Ryan, eventually acquired two nicknames: Rocky and Shaky.

Mitch and Vicki Schuster's baby was also born amid the chaos that morning. Vicki recalled, "It was so strange having contractions and aftershocks at the same time." Her son was born at 5 A.M. at a Woodland Hills hospital. One of the nurses asked what the couple would name him, and Mitch said, "What about Joshua?" after the biblical story in the Book of Joshua in which the walls of Jericho came tumbling down.

At California State University-Northridge, the closest university to the epicenter, a major parking structure and fifty-eight buildings sustained significant damage. The Oviatt Library suffered exterior and interior damage. Two students were killed. The Fine Arts Building and the South Library were so badly damaged that they had to be destroyed and replaced. The campus was closed, and the start of the next semester was delayed while the university underwent a $406-million recovery effort. Fortunately, because of strict state building codes, there was comparatively little damage to elementary and secondary schools in the area, although classes were suspended for several days.

Some quake damage had a surreal effect, like the parking garage at CSU-Northridge.
PHOTOGRAPH COURTESY OF THE U.S. GEOLOGICAL SURVEY.

In Hollywood, the quake disrupted the action at movie and television studios and sets. The Warner Brothers film, *Murder in the First*, was being shot only four miles from the epicenter. Production came to a halt. The building that housed the main courtroom set was in ruins and was red-tagged, so it was off limits. Jay Leno's *Tonight Show*, which filmed in Burbank close to the epicenter of the quake, had to be cancelled. A Wes Craven film, *New Nightmare*, contained earthquake scenes and was shot a month before the Northridge Earthquake. Some people involved in the film had been critical of the movie's earthquake sequences, claiming they were too drastic and unrealistic. A cameraman from the film ventured out to shoot actual footage of the Northridge quake and showed it to the Craven movie group. They no longer thought their earlier film footage had gone too far. In addition to current work being halted, there was also a loss of older, archived films and television episodes.

One unusual result of the earthquake was an outbreak of Valley Fever in Ventura. Valley Fever is a respiratory disease caused by inhaling the coccidiodes fungus. Of the 203 cases reported following the earthquake,

3 proved fatal. Health experts believed that the fungal spores were carried by dust created by the landslides from the earthquake; most of the cases occurred immediately downwind of the slides.

As a result of the tremendous losses of the Northridge Earthquake, most California homeowner-insurance companies stopped offering new policies that would cover losses due to earthquakes. The state created the California Earthquake Authority to provide basic residential earthquake coverage. After the earthquake, codes for construction of buildings and highways were improved.

As bad as the Northridge Earthquake was, it might have been worse. It happened early in the morning on a national holiday (Martin Luther King Jr. Day), so fewer people than usual were using the freeways. And steps had been taken after the Sylmar Earthquake of 1971 to strengthen building and safety codes.

The 6.6-magnitude Sylmar Earthquake had occurred at 6:02 A.M. on February 9, 1971. It lasted over a minute and had an epicenter at Northridge. It was noticed in Ventura, San Bernardino, and San Diego. During this quake, forty-nine people were killed at the Veterans Administration Hospital in San Fernando, where two buildings collapsed. Three additional deaths occurred at the Olive View Hospital in Sylmar: two patients died when they lost access to the constant stream of oxygen they required, and a staff member lost his life when he was hit by falling debris. Some of the buildings on the hospital grounds were completely destroyed. In one two-story building, the second floor collapsed onto the first floor, which was fortunately empty. Some stairwells constructed outside the buildings pulled away from the structures. Elsewhere, two people died when a section of the Golden State Freeway collapsed at its junction with the Antelope Valley Freeway. The Golden State Freeway suffered three collapsed sections and damage from rockslides. There was major damage to 1,300 buildings and 1,700 mobile homes. Another great concern was whether the Lower Van Norman Dam at Mission Hills would hold. It was an earth-filled concrete dam holding the largest reservoir in the city system at the time. Much of the concrete facing was crumbled by the quake, but the earthen core held.

The Sylmar Earthquake revealed that, in addition to the distant San Andreas Fault, there were widespread, previously unknown faults throughout the San Fernando Valley. This knowledge changed future quake-management efforts. Some improvements had been made prior to the Northridge Earthquake, but reconstruction of bridges and highways takes time and money.

Many lessons were learned from the Northridge Earthquake. The fault that caused the quake had been unknown. Efforts were immediately undertaken to find and map more of the region's faults. Researchers also learned how the soft Los Angeles soil magnified shaking during an earthquake. They provided this information in planning sessions to strengthen building codes. Many buildings and freeways in the area were identified as needing seismic retrofits, and officials have been addressing these as time and money allow. Early warning of an earthquake would be a big help, and a prototype system has been developed. State and federal funds are being sought to expand it. Los Angeles partnered with the U.S. Geological Survey, working closely with seismologist Lucy Jones, to create a comprehensive earthquake safety plan.

In spite of research and planning, it's an inescapable fact that California has fifty earthquakes a day. Most are imperceptible. With each tremor, the question always remains, "Is this the Big One?"

SOURCES

Earthquakes of December 1812

The 1812 Santa Barbara Earthquake in Brief. University of California–Santa Barbara.

Bancroft, Hubert Howe. *History of California, Vol. II, 1801–1824*. San Francisco, CA: The History Company, 1886.

Johnson, Paul C., editor. *The California Missions: A Pictorial History*. Menlo Park, CA: Lane Book Company, 1964.

Lozos, J. D. (2016) "A case for the historic joint rupture of the San Andreas and San Jacinto faults." *Science Advances*, American Association for the Advancement of Science, 2 (3): 196-199.

Pararas-Carayannis, George. The Santa Barbara, California Earthquakes and Tsunamis of December 1812: A study of historical tsunamis in California. Marina Advisors, U.S. Regulatory Agency and the U.S. Army Coastal Engineering Research Center.

Phillips, George Harwood. *Indians and Intruders in Central California, 1769–1849.* Norman, OK: University of Oklahoma Press, 1993.

Secrest, William B. Jr. and William B. Secrest Sr. *California Disasters, 1812–1899.* Sanger, CA: Word Dancer Press, 2006.

Wrightwood Earthquake. Southern California Earthquake Data Center, California Institute of Technology.

San Francisco Earthquake and Fire

Bronson, William. *The Earth Shook, the Sky Burned: A Photographic Account of the San Francisco Earthquake and Fire.* San Francisco, CA: Chronicle Books, Kindle ed., 2013.

Gerstle, Mark Lewis. *Memories.* Berkeley, CA: Bancroft Library, Online Archive of California.

Hansen, Richard and Gladys Hansen. *1906 San Francisco Earthquake.* Mt. Pleasant, SC: Arcadia Publishing, 2013.

Hoffman, Abraham. *California's Deadliest Earthquakes, A History.* Charleston, SC: The History Press, 2017.

"Jack London and the Great Earthquake and Fire." Virtual Museum of the City of San Francisco. http://www.sfmuseum.net/hist5/jlondon.html.

Kurzman, Dan. *Disaster! The Great San Francisco Earthquake and Fire.* New York, NY: Harper Perennial, 2002.

Lesser, Sol. *Reminiscences*: oral history, 1970. Columbia University Libraries Archival Collections. New York, NY: Oral History Research Office, Butler Library, Columbia University.

World Series Earthquake

Fifteen Seconds: The Great California Earthquake of 1989. San Francisco, CA: The Tides Foundation, Covelo, CA–Washington, D.C., Island Press, 1989.

Finrite, Ron. *Three Weeks in October: Three Weeks in the life of the Bay Area, the 1989 World Series and the Loma Prieta Earthquake,* produced in collaboration with the San Francisco Giants, Oakland Athletics, and Major League Baseball. Woodford Publishing, 1990.

Nakata, John K., Charles E. Meyer, Howard G. Wilshire, John C. Tinsley, William S. Updegrove, D. M. Peterson, Stephen D. Ellen, Ralph A. Haugerud, Robert J. McLaughlin, G. Reid Fisher, and Michael F. Diggles. *The October 17, 1989 Loma Prieta, California Earthquake, Selected Photographs.* U.S. Geological Survey, Digital Data Series DDS-29, Version 1.2, 1989.

Northridge Earthquake

Antczak, John. "Northridge quake thrashed Los Angeles 25 years ago this week." Associated Press. January 16, 2019.

Jones, Ray and Joe Lubow. *Disasters and Heroic Rescues of California.* Globe Pequot Press, 2006.

Martin, John A. and Associates. The Northridge Earthquake of 1/17/94 Parts I and II. Johnmartin.com. No date.

Martinez, Michael. "Six things we've learned since 1994 Northridge Earthquake." CNN. September 8, 2014.

"Northridge Earthquake: Readers Remember the Disaster Before Dawn." *Los Angeles Times.* January 14, 2014.

O'Brien, Catherine. "Severe quake hits Southern California, at least 24 dead." Associated Press. In AP Was There: California's deadly 1994 Northridge earthquake. January 16, 2019.

O'Brien, Paul W. *Social Response to the 1994 Northridge California Earthquake.* Submitted to the Natural Hazards Research and Applications Information Center, University of Colorado, Boulder, CO, 1994.

Reich, Kenneth. "Study Raises Northridge Quake Death Toll to 72." *Los Angeles Times.* December 20, 1995.

THE DONNER PARTY

MORE DEAD THAN ALIVE, MRS. MURPHY, A MEMBER OF THE DONNER Party wagon train, pushed herself upright in the freezing snow at a camp near Truckee Lake and asked an approaching rescue party, "Are you men from California, or do you come from Heaven?"

It was February 18, 1847. The Donner Party wagon train had set out for California from Missouri, in April 1846. The group had been trapped in the Sierra Nevada since October 28, 1846, freezing and starving and watching the men, women, and children of the party die one after another. What events led to this tragedy?

Each year, hundreds of wagon trains made the perilous journey west as people sought a better life, drawn by stories of abundant water and verdant valleys. Some, including members of the Donner Party, hoped that California's temperate climate would cure whatever ailments bedeviled them. Independence, Missouri, was often the gathering point from which these bold pioneers began their migration.

In the spring of 1846, the families of Jacob and George Donner, along with the family of James Reed, made up a three-wagon train that started west from Independence. In this group were sixty-year-old George and

James and Margaret Reed joined the Donner family
at the journey's start in Springfield, Illinois.
PHOTOGRAPH COURTESY OF THE BANCROFT LIBRARY. U.C. BERKELEY.

forty-four-year-old Tamsen Donner and their five children; fifty-six-year-old Jacob and forty-five-year-old Betsy Donner and their seven children; and forty-five-year-old James and thirty-two-year-old Margaret Reed, their four children, and Margaret's mother, seventy-year-old Sarah Keyes, who was very ill with tuberculosis. With the group were two servants and seven teamsters.

The Reed family had the most elaborate wagon in the group, a two-story affair. The other wagons were much simpler and were equipped for a journey of about four months. They left Independence on May 12, 1846.

Although the Oregon Trail was well established, some pioneers attempted more direct routes to California. Most of the pioneers traveling that year planned to take the Oregon Trail. A few groups were interested in a new route they had read about called the Hastings Cutoff. All of these groups were traveling in the direction of Fort Bridger in southwest

Wyoming. Within a week of leaving Independence, the Donners and Reeds joined a group of about fifty wagons.

While crossing Kansas, Mrs. Reed's elderly mother died and was buried beside the trail. The party reached Fort Laramie in present-day Wyoming on June 27, only a week behind schedule. There, James Reed met an old friend, James Clyman, traveling east from California. Clyman advised him not to take the Hastings Cutoff, saying it was barely walkable and wagons couldn't follow the trail. The friend recommended that the party take the established route to Oregon through Fort Hall in what today is southern Idaho.

After leaving Fort Laramie, the party met a rider with a message from Lansford Hastings advising the pioneers to go to Fort Bridger, where Hastings would meet them and guide them over the Cutoff. The Cutoff passed south of the Great Salt Lake, through Nevada along the Humboldt River, and then climbed into the Sierra Nevada along the Truckee River. They thought this would save them days or even weeks of travel. This persuaded Reed to disregard his friend's advice in favor of trying the new route.

Heading west, the wagon train reached the confluence of the Big and Little Sandy Rivers, west of South Pass and the Continental Divide. Here the trail split. Wagon trains could continue on the well-established trail north, headed for Oregon via the Snake and Columbia Rivers, or they could take a more southerly route to the Hastings Cutoff. Most took the established trail.

Others, including the Reeds and Donners, decided to take the Hastings Cutoff. They elected George Donner to be the captain of their wagon train. At this point, the Donner Party numbered about eighty-seven people. On reaching Fort Bridger, however, they learned that Hastings wasn't there. He had set off with another group but had left word that anyone interested in the Cutoff should follow and catch up with him.

The Donner Party headed off on the new trail to Weber Canyon. Hastings had written that this canyon would provide an easy way through the rugged Wasatch Mountains of Utah. For about a week, the party did well, traveling about ten or twelve miles a day. At the Weber River they came to a halt. Members of the Donner Party found a note from Hastings. It was attached to a stick, and it said that the path ahead was more difficult than he had expected. Hastings recommended that they wait there until he returned to lead them. The Donner Party made camp.

James Reed and two other men went ahead in search of Hastings. They found him five days later, but he refused to come back with them. Instead, he took Reed to the top of a hill and pointed out the trail they should take. Reed returned to the Donner Party with this information.

The party was uncertain what to do. They could return to the Little Sandy junction, but they would waste days retracing their path. Or they could continue west. The Donner Party set out again on the new route Hastings had advised, but they soon found it even harder than the Weber Canyon Trail. They were basically cutting a path through the forest and across rocky ground. Even though they were now behind schedule, they persisted and finally made it through the mountains to the Great Salt Lake.

They swung south of the lake and then crossed the vast salt flats, where they struggled for six days as wagons bogged down in briny mud. Oxen, crazed with thirst, broke free and ran off into the desert in search of water. Somehow the party made it to a freshwater spring where they rested before looping around the Ruby Mountains and heading north to meet the main route to California along the Humboldt River. It was September 26. The Cutoff had cost them a month, and they were far behind schedule. Despite their troubles, perhaps the most difficult leg of the journey was yet to come—crossing the high, rugged Sierra Nevada. That would be a struggle for a wagon train at the best of times, but snow would make the route impassable. In the mountains, winter was just around the corner.

Charles Stanton and William McCutchen left the Donner Party to ride ahead to Sacramento to try to obtain supplies for the group. George Donner and his family also separated from the wagon train and were a full day ahead of the main group. Then, on October 5, as the main party traveled along the Humboldt River, two wagon teams became entangled.

A man named John Snyder became angry and beat some of James Reed's oxen. Reed confronted Snyder, and the argument came to blows; Snyder hit Reed on the head, and in return Reed stabbed Snyder in the chest and killed him. Members of the Donner Party expelled Reed from the group. Reed and a teamster left the wagon train and set off for California with one horse between them.

These various problems and delays caused the Donner Party to reach the Sierras much later in the season than they had intended. Still, the settlers were not overly worried because they'd been advised that passes in the Sierras were usually open until mid-November. Some wanted to wait and rest, but others wanted to push on. The main party caught up with George and Tamsen Donner, and then, one by one, the wagons began the ascent into the mountains along the Truckee River. Bringing up the rear were the Donner brothers, George and Jacob.

Of course, throughout the trip there were illnesses and accidents. Five members of the party died before they reached campsites in the Sierras. One man, William Pike, was accidentally killed by a gunshot. When an axle broke on the Donner wagon, George Donner cut his hand while working on a piece of wood to repair it. All members of the group were weary and hungry as food supplies were low.

On October 19, Charles Stanton, along with two Miwok native guides, returned from Sutter's Fort on the west side of the Sierras, bringing mules and welcome food to the group. Stanton told them he had seen Reed on the way, that McCutchen was still in Sacramento recovering from the trip west, and that the pass should remain open for a few more weeks.

The first of the Donner Party wagons toiling up the steep mountains stopped and made camp at a lake about three miles from the summit pass. They found three widely separated, old cabins with dirt floors and flat leaky roofs. Another wagon from their party soon joined them.

A heavy snowfall began on October 28. Another wagon passed the first campers and continued on, trying to reach the summit, but this group gave up because the snow was soon so deep they couldn't find the trail. They turned back and joined the others. Within a day, all the families were camped together near Truckee Lake (now known as Donner Lake), except for a small group with the Donner brothers, who, because they had started last and had suffered a broken axle, were about five miles below them on the trail. The blizzard continued, and the pioneers realized they were trapped in a dangerous position. Soon the snow was six feet deep. They couldn't go forward or back.

As they settled into the Truckee Lake camp, one or two families moved into each of the three deserted cabins. One man built a lean-to for his family against one of the existing cabin walls. They patched the roofs as best they could to keep out the snow and rain. Of the sixty people who camped at the lake, nineteen were men over eighteen, twelve were women, and twenty-nine were children. Several miles down the trail near Alder Creek, the Donner brothers set up tents for twenty-one people, including six men, three women, and twelve children.

The trapped members of the Donner Party didn't know that James Reed, whom they had cast out, had reached Sacramento about two weeks earlier. There he met William McCutchen, who had recovered from his resupply trip with Stanton. John Sutter provided them with horses, supplies, and men to attempt a return trip to the Donner Party. This rescue party soon found that their horses could not negotiate the deep snow, so they continued on foot. Reed didn't really know where the Donner Party was at this time, but he

The party camped at Truckee Lake (now Donner Lake), shown here from the summit of Donner Pass in 1866. PHOTOGRAPH COURTESY OF THE LIBRARY OF CONGRESS, LC-USZ62-26948.

hoped they were on the west side of the summit. About twelve miles from the summit, the rescue party found the going too difficult. Seeing no sign of the Donner Party, they turned back to Sutter's Fort.

At the Truckee Lake and Alder Creek camps, members of the trapped Donner Party faced many snowstorms, some lasting for eight days. In some spots, the snow was soon twenty feet deep. Food supplies were running dangerously low. Several of the oxen died, and their frozen carcasses were stacked to be used as a source of food. One of the men went hunting and shot a bear, but after that he had no more luck. The lake wasn't yet frozen over, but no one knew how to fish in a lake.

Not knowing that Reed had made an unsuccessful rescue attempt to find them, the pioneers felt desperate. In the days that followed, three small parties tried to walk over the pass to go for help, but each failed and returned to camp. A larger group tried walking out on November 21 on makeshift snowshoes. This group reached the summit and went a short distance down the western side before giving up in deep snow and returning to camp on November 23.

Peter Breen was one of the pioneers who kept a diary noting the weather and other conditions. From notes and later verbal accounts, we know some information about how people survived in the camps. Although the cabins were extremely cramped, the weather was so bad that often the people couldn't go outside at all. Food at this point consisted mostly of soup made from the bones of oxen and horses that had died and small strips of ox hide that were boiled to make a kind of jelly. The Murphy family finally cooked and ate the ox-hide rug in their cabin. Occasionally a mouse came into one of the cabins and was promptly caught and eaten.

As people grew weaker and weaker, they spent most of their time in bed. Now and then, a few of the men at Truckee Lake would hike down to the Donner camp. They learned that three men had died from hunger and exposure and that George Donner's cut hand had become badly infected.

As days and weeks went on, the pioneers realized that they all faced starvation. Rather than sit and watch the children starve, a small group set off again in the snow to try to get help. They were gone for four days before they returned to camp. With nothing else to eat, they began to eat the ox hides that served as roofs to their cabins.

After two more men died, the pioneers at Truckee Lake realized that they needed to make another desperate attempt to get help and supplies. In mid-December, Franklin Graves made snowshoes. Seventeen people set off to try to get over the mountain pass to Bear Valley and on to Sacramento. On the first day, one man and a younger boy turned back, leaving nine men, including the two Miwok guides, five women, and one thirteen-year-old boy. They had scant rations for six days, not knowing that their trip would take a month.

Conditions were terrible, and all of the people who made up this snowshoe party were weak and in poor shape before they even set out. The snowshoes worked fairly well, but the snow was deep, which made for very slow going. Some members of the party soon became snow blind.

On the second day, they reached the summit. On the third day, there was another heavy snowstorm. On the sixth day, Charles Stanton decided not to continue on with the group but to stay behind and smoke his pipe. He was never seen again by the party.

According to some accounts, the decision was made among the snowshoe party to eat parts of three men who had died. Accounts vary, but some may have resorted to cannibalism while others didn't. Similar stories circulated about people in the Truckee Lake and Alder Creek camps resorting to cannibalism, or at least feeding parts of the dead to the youngest children.

On January 12, the seven survivors of the snowshoe party stumbled into a Miwok camp. The travelers looked so awful that at first the Native Americans fled from them. Then they offered the pioneers acorns and pine nuts, which were the only food they had. It had taken the pioneers thirty-three days to get to this point. After a few days of rest, a Miwok guided them to a ranch in a small farming community near the Sacramento

Valley. Only seven people from the snowshoe party survived—two adult men and all five women.

It was neither quick nor easy to organize a rescue party. The Mexican-American War was going on, and California settlements were in turmoil. The U.S. Army offered no support for a rescue effort. John Sutter called for volunteers, but only three men came forward. Then Sutter and John Sinclair offered $3 a day to anyone who would join a rescue crew. About a dozen men were willing to go. Sutter and Sinclair supplied provisions and animals.

It was early February when this rescue party set out from Johnson's Ranch (near today's town of Wheatland southeast of Yuba City) to find the emigrants at Truckee Lake and Alder Creek. The roads were muddy and swollen creeks were difficult to cross. After six days, they reached snowline, and the mules couldn't manage further travel. One man went back to Sutter's Fort with the tired animals. Two men stayed with some supplies, which they cached. The others continued, each carrying about fifty pounds. They cached more of their supplies along the way to lighten their loads. After five days, three of the men refused to proceed. A leader of the group offered $5 a day for anyone who would finish the rescue effort.

These stumps cut by the Donner Party show the depth of the snow during the encampment.
PHOTOGRAPH BY LAWRENCE AND HOUSEWORTH, COURTESY OF THE LIBRARY OF CONGRESS, LC-USZ62-27607.

The first of the rescue party reached the Truckee Lake camp on February 17. Three of the rescuers hiked down to the Donner camp at Alder Creek and returned with four children and three adults, leaving the others there in poor shape. The rescuers then took twenty-four members of the Donner Party—those they thought were strong enough to walk out and for whom they had sufficient food—and began the trek back to Sacramento, leaving what supplies they could for the thirty-one who remained.

Meanwhile, James Reed was busy raising money to mount another rescue party. He took in $1,300, plus a $100 donation from the government. He organized a second relief party that left Johnson's Ranch late in February. When they reached the snowline, they had to take the supplies off the horses and continue on foot. They met up with the first rescue party on its way back to Sacramento. Reed was briefly reunited with his wife and two of his children who were in that group.

Reed's party continued on to the camps at Truckee Lake and Alder Creek. Then the rescuers started the trip back, bringing seventeen people, mostly children, and leaving very few in the camp. During their return trip, another heavy snowstorm struck. Most of the weakened pioneers couldn't go on and were left in a temporary camp while Reed continued out with a few others. When rescuers came back for the pioneers left in camp, three had died and the rest were finally brought out.

A third relief party arrived on March 14 and found seven survivors, among them George and Tamsen Donner and Lewis Keseberg. Keseberg was too weak to travel. George was too ill from his infected hand to move, and Tamsen refused to leave George. The rescuers took four children with them back to Sacramento.

On April 10, a salvage party arrived at Truckee Lake seeking anything of value they could sell in Sacramento to raise money to help support the orphaned children. The salvage party found only Keseberg alive in the camp, and he was brought to Sutter's Fort on April 17, the last survivor of the tragic Donner Party. George and Tamsen Donner were dead. Of the eighty-seven who began the journey, forty-five survived.

Louis "Lewis" Keseberg was the last of the Donner Party to be rescued. He became a successful owner of a restaurant and brewery in Sacramento.
PHOTOGRAPH COURTESY OF THE BANCROFT LIBRARY, U.C. BERKELEY.

43

Martha "Patty" Reed Lewis, the oldest child of James and Margaret Reed,
was eight years old at the time. She settled with her family in San Jose,
later married Frank Lewis, and had eight children.
PHOTOGRAPH CIRCA 1920, COURTESY OF HISTORY SAN JOSE.

News of the tragedy quickly spread and reached the East Coast by
summer 1847, but the discovery of gold at Sutter's Mill barely six months
later jump-started the California gold rush. The plight of the Donner
Party was soon a mere afterthought for thousands of prospectors headed
west to seek their fortunes. But the name lives on: Truckee Lake became
Donner Lake and the pass just to its west is now Donner Pass.

SOURCES

Burns, Ric. *The American Experience: The Donner Party.* PBS Video. 1992.

EyeWitnesstoHistory.com. *The Tragic Fate of the Donner Party.* Ibis
Communications, Inc.

Kaufman, Richard K. *Saving the Donner Party and Forlorn Hope.* New York, NY:
Archway Press, 2014.

McGlashan, C. F. *History of the Donner Party: A Tragedy of the Sierras.* Stanford, CA:
Stanford University Press, 1947.

Rarick, Ethan. *Desperate Passage: The Donner Party's Perilous Journey.* New York, NY:
Oxford University Press, 2008.

Stewart, George R. *Ordeal by Hunger: The Donner Party.* New York, NY: Houghton
Mifflin, 1992, p. 191.

SHIP WRECKS AND EXPLOSIONS

WATERCRAFT HAVE BEEN AN IMPORTANT FORM OF TRANSPORTATION throughout California's history, perhaps even dating back to the first people to arrive, coming down the coast from the Bering land bridge in paleolithic times. Certainly, early indigenous people used canoes made of dugout trees, sewn planks, or bundled tule stalks to navigate coastal waters as well as inland bays, rivers, and lakes.

In 1542, conquistador Juan Cabrillo sailed two ships along the coast of what would become the state of California, the first Europeans to do so. Cabrillo and his crews may have sailed as far north as Point Reyes before turning south. English explorer Francis Drake followed in 1579, landing in Drakes Bay at today's Point Reyes National Seashore. Drake mapped and labeled prominent coastal features, including an exposed reef near present-day Crescent City that features in one of this chapter's stories.

Russian fur traders and U.S. ship merchants plied these waters in the late 1700s and early 1800s, but the start of the gold rush in 1848 brought an exponential increase in shipping traffic. The stories that follow detail some of the more dramatic ship wrecks and explosions.

PADDLE WHEELER EXPLOSIONS, 1850S TO 1880S

In the middle and late 1800s, the waters of San Francisco Bay teemed with steamship traffic, especially paddle wheelers. Paddleboats crisscrossed the bay and went up the Sacramento River to Sacramento and on to the Yuba and Feather Rivers. Some paddleboats traveled the San Joaquin River as far as Stockton. They carried both passengers and freight. The steam boilers in these paddleboats were a great source of energy, but they were also very dangerous. From 1850 to 1888, there were at least eighteen steamboat explosions, with fatalities ranging from two to over fifty deaths in each incident.

The first steamboat to appear in the Sacramento Delta was the *Sitka*, which in November 1847 made its way up the Sacramento River to John Sutter's settlement. This ship was only thirty-seven feet long, and it took more than six days to make the journey. The *Sitka* had been in service in Alaska. It had since been taken apart, shipped to Yerba Buena Island in San Francisco Bay, and reassembled. Soon, larger paddle wheelers arrived in San Francisco Bay. Many of these were brought to San Francisco from the East Coast.

Paddle wheeler steamships, like the sidewheeler *El Capitan* shown here docking in San Francisco circa 1870, provided critical passenger and freight transport until bridge and rail systems replaced them.
PHOTOGRAPH BY THOMAS HOUSEWORTH & CO.,
COURTESY OF NEW YORK PUBLIC LIBRARY DIGITAL COLLECTION.

In addition to the large steamships, there were many smaller ones that hauled freight and passengers up the smaller rivers. Many of these paddleboats were less than 100 feet from bow to stern. They went up the Sacramento River as far as Red Bluff and Redding. During spring runoff, they could go up the San Joaquin River nearly to Fresno. They also navigated up the Tuolumne, Stanislaus, Feather, American, and Yuba Rivers. Sometimes the water was so shallow that passengers had to get out and help dig their vessel off a sandbar.

Soon there were enough boats that competition for passengers drove the price of travel very low. There was also a push for speed. Sometimes one steamship raced another, with the passengers cheering them on. Settlements grew along the waterways, and steamships became a dependable means of travel. But such travel was not without danger, and this danger increased when ships went faster and faster. Between 1850 and 1898, an estimated 270 people were killed in steamship explosions.

THE STEAMSHIP *SAGAMORE*, 1851

On September 9, 1851, California was admitted as a state into the Union. It took days for the news to travel to San Francisco from Washington, D.C., where President Millard Fillmore had signed the bill. On October 29, celebrations were going on in the city to commemorate the great news. There were parades, balls, feasts, and many firework displays.

Shortly after 5 P.M., while the steamship *Sagamore* was pulling away from the Central Wharf in San Francisco to begin a trip to Stockton, its boiler exploded. Timbers and bodies were blown far and wide. The master of the ship, Captain Cole, was thrown fifty feet into the water. Although he suffered injuries, he survived. The cause of the explosion was thought to be insufficient water in the boiler. The *Sagamore* had been built just two months earlier at a cost of $60,000. It was the first steamship to have been built right in San Francisco. Its boilers had been built in a foundry in South Boston.

People onshore and in nearby boats came to the rescue. Even when the *Sagamore* had sunk as low as it could go, men dove into the water, swam to the ship, and searched through cabins trying to rescue additional victims. About eighty-five people were on board and forty-five died in the explosion. As if one disaster weren't enough, some of the injured were taken to a hospital that caught fire during the night. All of the hospital's 130 patients were evacuated, though several of the *Sagamore* casualties suffered additional trauma.

THE STERNWHEELER *JENNY LIND*, 1853

From South Bay, there was daily paddleboat service from San Jose's Port of Alviso to San Francisco. The trip took about eight hours. The *Jenny Lind*, a sternwheeler, was a fairly small ship, allowing it to navigate the narrow Alviso Slough. It carried about 150 passengers and was an hour faster and considerably more comfortable than taking a stagecoach from San Jose to San Francisco. The boat was named after Jenny Lind, an opera singer popular at the time who was promoted by P. T. Barnum and known as "the Swedish Nightingale."

Just after noon on April 11, 1853, the *Jenny Lind* was in San Francisco Bay just offshore of what is now Palo Alto, making its way to San Francisco. Just as many of the passengers were sitting down to lunch, a tremor shook the boat, followed by an ear-splitting explosion. A plate on the ship's boiler blew off. Witnesses heard a terrible roar as scalding steam and parts of the exploding engine sailed through the air. Thirty-one passengers and crew were killed, and at least nineteen others were injured. Since the passenger list was incomplete, an accurate accounting isn't available. Among those killed that day were Jacob Hoppe, a founder of the *Daily Alta California* newspaper and signer of the California constitution; Charles White, mayor of San Jose; and Thomas Godden, a prominent landowner and attorney.

Many in the dining room were killed by scalding water and flying debris. One passenger, James Tobin, who had previously traveled by steamboat on the Mississippi River, recognized the signs of impending danger. He covered himself with his cape and dropped immediately to the deck after the first tremor. He received only minor burns, while the unsuspecting man next to him was killed. People on deck near the rail jumped or were thrown overboard. One was picked up, while as many as twelve may have drowned.

The boat dropped anchor and a passenger swam to shore for aid. A sailboat and several other small boats came to help. A nearby steamer, the *Union*, seeing the *Jenny Lind*'s flag

Among the victims of the *Jenny Lind* explosion was newspaper owner Jacob D. Hoppe, a signer of the California constitution.
PHOTOGRAPH IN PUBLIC DOMAIN.

flying upside down to signal its distress, came alongside and picked up both injured and uninjured passengers.

When news of the explosion reached San Francisco, the mayor began planning for the casualties. The owner of the *Jenny Lind* chartered the steamer *Cape Kearney* and equipped it with medical supplies and several doctors. The *Kearney* set off shortly after 9 P.M. and met the *Union* an hour later. Physicians boarded the *Union* to aid the injured. On reaching San Francisco, passengers were taken to rooms in various hotels and rooming houses.

This disaster, in which a number of prominent citizens were killed, increased awareness of the danger of steamship travel and ultimately spurred the building of a railroad from San Jose to San Francisco. Today, a memorial plaque to honor the victims stands in Alviso Marina County Park in Santa Clara County.

That same year, two steamship explosions occurred on the same day, October 18, 1853. The *American Eagle*, coming down from Stockton, blew up at 3:30 A.M. Then at 5 P.M., the *Stockton* exploded going upriver from San Francisco. A total of seven people died in the two explosions.

THE STEAMSHIP *SECRETARY*, 1854

On April 15, 1854, the *Secretary*, helmed by Captain Travis, left Pacific Wharf at about 10 A.M. carrying sixty-five passengers north to Petaluma. The steamship *Nevada* left for Petaluma about fifteen minutes later. The *Nevada* caught up with the *Secretary*, and the two ships began to race. Such racing was not uncommon and was often encouraged by the passengers.

The *Secretary*'s boiler exploded as the ship passed between two pairs of islands known as The Brothers and The Sisters. At this point, the *Nevada* was about 100 yards ahead of the *Secretary*, and fragments of the exploding *Secretary* flew onto it. No fewer than fifteen of the *Secretary*'s passengers flew into the water, sank, and were never seen again. The *Nevada* immediately stopped to offer help. It rescued thirty-eight people who were treading water. One body was pulled out of the water. A few of the survivors were uninjured, but most had burns and broken bones. The *Nevada* returned to port in San Francisco, where doctors assisted the injured.

At an inquest following the incident, survivors testified that Captain Travis had said he intended to race his ship against the *Nevada*, aiming to reach Petaluma two or three hours ahead of it. One passenger said he had seen an oar tied over the lever of the safety valve, blocking its use. Even though these statements suggested negligence or incompetence on the part of the captain and crew, no legal action was pursued. The *Secretary* had been on this run to Petaluma for about two months. It had new boilers, but its engine had previously been used on the steamer *Sagamore*.

The *Chrysopolis* was a finely appointed and fast ship running
between San Francisco and Sacramento.
PHOTOGRAPH COURTESY OF THE ONLINE ARCHIVE OF CALIFORNIA.

THE DEADLY *WASHOE*, 1864

The deadliest Bay Area steamer accident occurred September 5, 1864,
when the *Washoe* exploded on the Sacramento River just above Rio Vista
on a trip from San Francisco to Sacramento. The *Washoe* carried 153
passengers from San Francisco and would pick up others at Benecia and
Rio Vista. It left port shortly after the steamers *Yosemite*, *Antelope*, and
Chrysopolis. After what seemed like a short race, the *Chrysopolis* pulled far
ahead of the others, while the heavily loaded *Antelope* fell far behind.

The *Chrysopolis* was a luxury ship built in San Francisco in 1860. It was
245 feet long, carried 1,000 passengers, and cost $200,000 to build. On
December 31, 1861, it had set a speed record for the journey from Sacramento
to San Francisco of five hours and nineteen minutes. The *Antelope* was also a
fine ship, the pride of the Steam and Navigation Company.

The *Washoe* proceeded to stop at Benecia and Rio Vista. Shortly after
the latter stop, it exploded and ran ashore. The forward deck of the *Washoe*

was on fire in three places. Some passengers were on the boat, some in the water, and some had made it to shore. Many were horribly burned. The captain and the two river pilots in the pilot house were uninjured. The *Antelope* arrived about two hours after the explosion. It took on about eighty victims—dead, injured, and uninjured. The passenger list was lost, so an accurate count couldn't be made. An estimated seventy-five to over eighty people died in the disaster.

Investigators believed that the explosion was caused by poor-quality iron used in the boiler. The captain and crew were said to have behaved admirably. The captain remained on board until all the dead and wounded were removed, and he contributed $1,000 to a relief fund.

This was not the last boiler explosion on a steam-powered paddle wheeler in the Sacramento Delta, but the number of explosions decreased as better boilers were built. The number of steamships carrying passengers and freight increased until the Civil War. Gradually, the paddle wheelers went out of use. The building of railroads, the development of cars and trucks, and the growing network of roads and bridges all played their part in the demise of paddle-wheel traffic.

As they went out of service, many of the old paddle wheelers were simply left at docks near Stockton and San Francisco. Some were used as clubhouses. Some were converted to barges and used to transport goods from farms and ranches along the rivers. Sometimes the engines and boilers of the old paddle wheelers were removed and put into cargo barges.

A few paddle wheelers remained in use into the twentieth century. In 1926, the *Delta Queen* and the *Delta King* were built, their steel hulls made in Scotland. The ships were finished in Stockton. Each was 250 feet long. They had elegant rooms, promenade decks, and luxurious dining rooms. On alternate days, they made round-trips from San Francisco to Sacramento with side trips to Stockton. But the calamitous heyday of passenger steamships was over. Service to Stockton ceased in 1932. All service ended in 1941.

THE WRECK OF THE *BROTHER JONATHAN*, 1865

On July 30, 1865, the paddle wheeler *Brother Jonathan* was struggling in storm-tossed seas to return to the safe harbor of the bay at Crescent City on the Northern California coast. Captain DeWolf had aborted the ship's journey north to Portland, Oregon, due to enormous swells and slow progress. The safety of the Crescent City breakwater was only six miles distant.

A crewman ran forward to ready the anchor for their anticipated arrival at Crescent City. Just then he spied an uncharted rock jutting from the sea. Before he could shout a warning, the next wave lifted the ship and dropped it right onto the sharp rock, which pierced the hull and ripped it open. A second wave drove the ship farther onto the reef, tearing up its hull. Almost immediately, Captain DeWolf knew there was no way to save the vessel. In fact, it would sink in forty-five minutes. He called everyone aft and cried, "Try to save yourselves."

The sinking of the *Brother Jonathan* remains one of the worst nautical disasters in California history. It resulted in the greatest loss of life in state maritime history. The events that led to this terrifying moment began when the ship was built in New York and launched in November 1850. Edward Mills, a New York banker, paid $190,000 to have it built. He planned to use this ship to make his fortune by capitalizing on the hordes of people who wanted to reach California and stake their claim in the gold rush.

In that era, there were three main ways to get to California from the eastern United States. Many came overland by foot, horse, or covered wagon. Some sailed on fast clipper ships from the eastern seaboard, around Cape Horn, and then up the coast to San Francisco. A third route was to sail to Panama, cross the Isthmus of Panama through the jungle via small boats and mule train, and then take a ship up the coast to San Francisco.

As originally built, *Brother Jonathan* was 220 feet long and 36 feet wide. It had upper and lower decks, with two 70-foot salons and berths for 365 passengers. It carried two masts and a 400-horsepower steam engine driving two side-mounted paddle wheels, each thirty-three feet in diameter. Its name was a popular personification of New England and an emblem of the United States in general, like Yankee Doodle or Uncle Sam.

The *Brother Jonathan* was to run from New York to Havana, Cuba, then to Kingston, Jamaica, and across the Gulf of Mexico to Charges (now Colon), Panama. There, the cargo and passengers would be off-loaded for the trip across the isthmus to the Pacific, and new cargo and passengers from San Francisco would board for the return trip to New York. On its first journey, stopping only at Kingston on the way back to New York, the *Brother Jonathan* set a new record by making the round-trip in thirty-one days.

At least three shipping companies competed for moving passengers and freight from one coast to the other by crossing the Isthmus of Panama. One of these companies belonged to Cornelius Vanderbilt, who had become wealthy running steamboats in the region around New York City. He was known as "The Commodore," a nickname based on the highest rank in the U.S. Navy at the time. Vanderbilt bought the *Brother Jonathan* outright and had the ship rebuilt with an extra mast and accommodations for more passengers.

This illustration portrays the *Brother Jonathan* after the ship was retrofitted with an extra mast and expanded cabin space.
IMAGE IN PUBLIC DOMAIN.

With 288 passengers, the *Brother Jonathan* left New York in June 1852, went around Cape Horn, up the west coast of South America, and on to San Francisco. The trip took 144 days. Over the next few years, different companies struggled to wrest control of the profitable shipping business. In 1858, Vanderbilt sold the *Brother Jonathan* to Captain John T. Wright, who renamed it, ironically, the *Commodore*, and put the ship on a regular run between San Francisco and Seattle with stops at Portland and Vancouver, Washington, on the Columbia River. Many of the passengers were gold prospectors.

By 1861, the *Commodore* was leaking and in poor shape. It sat at a dock in San Francisco and was bought by the California Steamship Navigation Company. For the next seven months, it underwent extensive repairs and remodeling. Passenger cabins were fitted out in California redwood. The number of cabins was greatly reduced so that it could carry 850 tons of cargo. And it was given back its old name, *Brother Jonathan*. On December 19, 1861, it returned to service.

From 1862 to 1865, the *Brother Jonathan* was one of the best-known steamships traveling the West Coast. It established a record time of sixty-nine hours one way between San Francisco and Portland. It made a fortune for its owners.

Captain DeWolf took over the *Brother Jonathan* in June 1865. Under his helm, the ship collided with a sailing ship, the *Jane Falkenberg*, on the Columbia River, damaging the *Brother Jonathan*'s hull. Upon its return to San Francisco, the captain recommended that the *Brother Jonathan* be hauled out of the water and repaired. Instead, the company decided to do the work at the dock.

By late July, the *Brother Jonathan* was ready for its next outing, bound again for Portland. One version of the story says that Captain DeWolf wasn't satisfied with the hull repairs, and he also objected to the amount of cargo being loaded for the upcoming trip. According to this account, an ore crusher weighing several tons had been loaded aboard and placed directly over the repaired section of hull. DeWolf noted that the ship was sitting too low in the water, and the passengers had yet to board. The shipping agent dismissed the captain's complaints and said he would hire another captain if necessary. The *Brother Jonathan*, he said, would sail with its cargo and passengers as soon as possible.

Whether the ship was overloaded remains speculation. No records are known to exist that corroborate this version of events, and it seems unlikely that Captain DeWolf would have agreed to sail such an overburdened vessel.

In any case, by July 28 the loading was finished. In addition to the cargo, the ship carried 54 crew members and 190 passengers, including the commander of the U.S. Army's newly created Department of Columbia (the Northwest), General George Wright, and his wife; the newly appointed governor of Washington Territory, Anson Henry; and James Nesbit, editor of the *San Francisco Evening Bulletin*. The *Brother Jonathan* was also carrying an unusually large amount of money. Major Eddy, a U.S. Army paymaster, had with him an estimated $200,000 in paper currency to pay troops at various Northwest posts. Also, William Logan, a government Indian agent, came aboard with gold coins to be used as annual treaty payments to various tribes on reservations. Additional crates of gold were loaded for personal business transactions, including some for Wells Fargo bank. Finally, two camels bound for an Oregon circus were on board.

Sticking with the "overloaded" version of the story, at noon on July 28, the *Brother Jonathan* was ready to go, but it couldn't move. It was so heavily laden that the bottom of the ship was stuck in the mud. The crew waited for an afternoon tide and used a tug to help them get started. Finally, the vessel headed north in high seas, with the weather growing rougher as it sailed. At 2 A.M. on July 30, the *Brother Jonathan* pulled into the harbor at Crescent City to offload a small amount of cargo. By 9 A.M., it was underway again, but the storm was building. It took two hours to go about fourteen miles, and the seas were worsening. Captain DeWolf decided to turn back and wait out the storm in Crescent City.

Rocks dot the ocean off the coast near Crescent City
looking northwest toward St. George Reef.
PHOTOGRAPH COURTESY OF ELLIN BELTZ.

This section of the Northern California coastline was known to be dangerous. There were frequent storms and strong currents to deal with. At Seal Rock, the captain plotted his course and headed for the Crescent City breakwater. But he had not cleared St. George Reef, a scattering of sharp spires rising 250 feet from the ocean floor that Sir Francis Drake had called "Dragon Rocks" when he sailed this stretch of coast in 1579. Waves smashed the *Brother Jonathan*'s hull onto these rocky teeth, and the ship began to sink.

The *Brother Jonathan* carried four iron "Francis Patent Metallic" lifeboats and two smaller wooden surfboats. Together, they could carry 250 people, but the fierce storm and instability of the foundering ship made launching the lifeboats almost impossible. Twenty-foot swells came crashing over the deck.

The first iron lifeboat that was launched immediately capsized. A second was launched, but the wind smashed it against the hull of the ship. The third mate decided to try one of the wooden surfboats. He managed to get five women, three children, and ten crewmen into the boat with him.

As they lowered it, the storm again swung the surfboat against the ship, damaging it slightly, but this boat stayed afloat. As its passengers struggled toward shore, they watched the *Brother Jonathan* sink beneath the waves. Three hours later, the surfboat reached the shore at Crescent City.

Four ships tried to go out to rescue the passengers of the *Brother Jonathan*, but all were turned back by the fierce storm as soon as they passed the breakwater. The storm raged on, and it was two days before anyone could make it out to the collision site. Except for the nineteen people in the third mate's small surfboat, there were no survivors. The other 225 passengers and crew drowned. The two circus camels also drowned. It was the worst maritime disaster in California history.

While the lifeboats were being loaded, one person was thinking ahead. James Nesbit, the editor of the *San Francisco Evening Bulletin*, was quickly writing a last will and testament with notes to his family. He wrapped the document in oilskin and fastened it to his body. In the days and weeks after the wreck, flotsam and a total of 185 bodies came ashore along the coast from Cape Sebastian, Oregon, to Trinidad Head, California. Nesbit's body and his oilskin-wrapped document were recovered.

Among the passengers who were lost were Daniel and Polina Rowell and their four children. They were traveling from Iowa to join Polina's parents in Oregon. Polina's father found his daughter and son-in-law washed up on the coast. He also claimed the bodies of four children, though he couldn't be sure they were his grandchildren, and buried them as a family.

But the sinking of the *Brother Jonathan* was not the end of the story. The wreck had far-reaching consequences. For one thing, the ship's reported cargo of gold drew treasure hunters to search for the wreckage, which ultimately led to its discovery more than a century later.

More crucially for shipping on this stretch of coast, two years after the wreck of the *Brother Jonathan*, the U.S. Lighthouse Board requested funds to build a lighthouse at St. George Reef on Northwest Seal Rock. Since the Civil War had only recently ended, funds were scarce and the project wasn't authorized. Two years later, Charles Ballantyne and George Gillespie Jr. completed the Tillamook Rock Lighthouse in Oregon, proving that it was possible to construct a lighthouse on such a difficult rock outcropping. Congress then allocated $50,000 for Ballantyne to survey Northwest Seal Rock, the outermost rock in St. George Reef, as the possible base of a lighthouse. Although the rock is only 300 feet in diameter and rises barely 50 feet above the waterline, Ballantyne envisioned blasting a stepped foundation for a stout base, or caisson, and a tower. Congress authorized $100,000 to start building the St. George Reef Lighthouse.

In April 1883, the schooner *La Ninfa* was towed into place and moored to Northwest Seal Rock. It would serve as barracks and mess hall for the crews building the lighthouse. A cable was attached from the schooner to the top of the rock, and a platform was suspended from it. The crew used this platform to get back and forth to work. The workmen would lash their tools to iron rings set in the rock to protect them from being washed away during stormy weather. Powerful explosives were used to blast away chunks of the rock, and by September the crew had created a terraced area on which to build.

ST. GEORGE'S REEF LIGHT STATION.
View from the South-West, showing the Rock as it appeared at the End of the Working Season, and the Method of Landing Men from the Schooner "La Ninfa"

This 1884 sketch by Paul J. Pelz depicts the cable used to carry workers between *La Ninfa* and the lighthouse construction site.
PHOTOGRAPH OF THE ILLUSTRATION COURTESY OF THE LIBRARY
OF CONGRESS, LC-DIG-PPMSCA-09358.

Because of storms and crashing seawater, work on the lighthouse could be carried out only in spring and summer. But during the winter months, Ballantyne learned of a granite deposit near Humboldt Bay. He arranged with the Mad River Railroad to transport granite blocks to the northern spit of Humboldt Bay, where he built a depot to store them. Quarrymen shaped the blocks to exacting dimensions so they would fit tightly together, presenting a near-seamless face to the sea. Then the granite was moved by ship to the reef, where a derrick and boom lifted the six-ton blocks onto Seal Rock. Congress provided only small amounts of funding over the next three years, so construction progress was minimal.

As Congress supplied more funding over the next decade, crews continued working on the lighthouse. As many as fifty-two men worked at a time on the project. The final appropriation from Congress, which brought the total cost of the lighthouse to $791,000 (about $21 million today) was made in December 1890. The St. George Reef Lighthouse was the most expensive lighthouse in the United States. On May 13, 1891, workers completed the fortress-like lighthouse tower. The rest of that work season was spent taking down the scaffolding, installing the lantern room atop the tower, and putting in a spiral staircase. It took another year for a Fresnel lens to arrive from France. A twelve-inch steam whistle was used as a foghorn. The St. George Reef Lighthouse was lit for the first time on October 20, 1892. It flashed every fifteen seconds, alternating red and white. The first head keeper of the light was a man who had worked on the lighthouse construction crew.

Due to its remote and exposed location, the St. George Reef Lighthouse was among the most dangerous posts in the country. Supplies and crew changes would come by launch, and the entire boat would be lifted by the boom onto a landing on the rock. More than once, this process went awry and men were killed. Waves could strike the rock from any direction, and during big storms they sometimes crashed over the top of the caisson, about seventy feet high. In one monstrous storm in 1952, a wave smashed

The St. George Reef Lighthouse stands exposed to the elements
on Northwest Seal Rock, six miles off the coast.
PHOTOGRAPH COURTESY OF ANITA RITENOUR, CC BY 2.0.

the lantern-room windows 144 feet above sea level, and seawater poured down the tower's interior spiral staircase.

Radiotelephones were installed at the lighthouse in October 1923, finally providing reliable communication with the mainland. The U.S. Lighthouse Service staffed the station until 1939, when the U.S. Coast Guard took over. Finally, in 1975, the lighthouse was decommissioned and replaced by a large navigational buoy. During the lighthouse's eighty-three years of operation, five keepers lost their lives while on duty. Chief Petty Officer James W. Sebastian made the final entry in the lighthouse logbooks:

It is with much sentiment that I pen this final entry, 13 May 1975. After four score and three years, St. George Reef Light is dark. No longer will your brilliant beams of light be seen, nor your bellowing fog signal be heard by the mariner. Gone are your keepers. Only by your faithful service has many a disaster been prevented on the treacherous St. George Reef. You stand today, as you have down through the years, a tribute to humanity and worthy of our highest respect. Cut from the soul of our country, you have valiantly earned your place in American history. In your passing, the era of the lonely sea sentinel has truly ended. May Mother Nature show you mercy. You have been abandoned, but never will you be forgotten. Farewell, St. George Reef Light.

Still, the saga of the sinking of the *Brother Jonathan* was not over. The gold coins reported to be in the sunken ship called irresistibly to treasure hunters. On October 1, 1993, after at least forty-five failed attempts by other searchers, Deep Sea Research consortium (DSR), succeeded in finding the wreckage of the *Brother Jonathan*. The ship was in murky waters, 260 feet down and about eight miles northwest of Crescent City. The salvage crew used a mini-submersible called *Snooper*. On their first foray, they took a few items, including a wine bottle and a medicine bottle, as proof that they had found the old paddle wheeler so they could lay salvor's claim to ownership in federal district court.

But exactly where in this wreckage was the gold? It took another three years of searching to confirm that treasure was actually on board. Gold coins were scattered on the ocean floor. A total of 1,207 coins in varying conditions were recovered. Now a new question arose. Did the gold belong to the salvagers or to the State of California? It would take a long court battle to decide ownership. A major figure in the court case was David Flohr of El Cajon, a retired Navy pilot and a partner in DSR. The consortium members asserted that they had undertaken this search for profit and had already spent about $1 million. They believed any treasure they found belonged to them.

On the other side of the case, in addition to the State of California, friend-of-the-court briefs were filed by fourteen other states and ten historical preservation societies. California was trying to establish precedent for future finds along its 1,000-mile coastline, pitting California law against federal law and the traditional rights of salvagers. California asserted this claim in the interest of preserving history. The *Brother Jonathan* would serve as a test case.

When lower courts didn't find for the State of California, the case was appealed to the U.S. Supreme Court, but the high court insisted that the facts of the case would need to be decided in a lower court. The State of California promised to keep its claims alive, and it became clear that a compromise would have to be reached by both sides if the litigation were ever to end.

After five and a half years, the case was finally settled in March 1999. It was agreed that the salvage company could keep 1,006 gold coins that its crews had found, could continue to retrieve what they could from the wreckage, and could keep 80 percent of that. The coins—$5, $10, and $20 gold pieces—were auctioned off in May 1999 in Los Angeles. The profits from the sale, which brought in $6.3 million, were to be divided among 100 small investors.

Under the settlement, the California Lands Commission would receive 20 percent of what was salvaged and would have a representative on board during future recovery missions to oversee historic preservation. The coins belonging to the Lands Commission were to be given to various museums. The salvage group held out hope that additional gold bullion, and perhaps a ship's safe containing paper money, might still be found. So the story of the sinking of the *Brother Jonathan* may not yet be over.

PORT CHICAGO MUNITIONS EXPLOSIONS, 1944

On a peaceful summer night in the Bay Area, just after ten in the evening, the pilot of a small airplane was flying at about 9,000 feet when suddenly the world below erupted into a huge ring of fire. Debris flew through the air. A piece of white-hot metal that the pilot described as "big as a house" hurtled by. Below, flames glowed yellow and orange. Smoke billowed upward for nearly two miles. It was July 17, 1944, with World War II in full spate, and the pilot had flown over Port Chicago, where a ship full of war munitions had just exploded.

As battles in the Pacific raged on, the U.S. Navy worked night and day to provide the necessary flow of war supplies, which included enormous amounts of bombs, artillery shells, depth charges, and small-arms ammunition. When the Naval Ammunition Depot at Mare Island in Suisun Bay couldn't fully supply the war effort, the Navy developed a munitions facility at Port Chicago, about thirty miles northeast of San Francisco. The site had a deepwater port and rail connections, and it was far from highly populated areas. Construction began in 1942.

During the summer of 1944, crews at Port Chicago worked around the clock, sometimes loading two ships at once. There were 1,432 enlisted men stationed at Port Chicago and 71 Navy officers. The base was guarded by 106 Marines. The enlisted sailors were African Americans; the officers and Marines were white.

Handling munitions on ships was laborious and dangerous work. For shifts at the pier, the sailors divided into groups of about twenty men each. Half of each team entered one of the five hatches of the ship while the other half remained on the dock. Boxcars of explosives ran on rails directly onto the pier beside the ship. In a boxcar, there might be wooden crates of ammunition or rows of bombs. Men would open the boxcar door, set up a plank, and then roll each 500-pound bomb onto the pier. These bombs didn't have detonators installed, but the men hung mattresses from the side of the ship in case a bomb got away and hit the ship, a common enough occurrence. The bombs and ammunition crates were placed in a net that was then hoisted by deck-mounted or mobile winches and lowered

Loading munitions at Port Chicago was dangerous work.
PHOTOGRAPH FROM THE U.S. DEPARTMENT OF DEFENSE,
COURTESY OF THE NATIONAL PARK SERVICE.

down the hatches to the men below. The men in the hold stacked the bombs and cases of ammunition in layers, one upon another. The top layer of the hold was reserved for stacking the incendiary bombs, which were 650-pound "hot" bombs with fuses already installed.

At Port Chicago, the sailors assigned to loading munitions served in African-American units segregated from white units. These men had minimal training in loading ships and even less in handling munitions. The schedule was so rushed that officers gave little priority to safety procedures and winch maintenance. Officers also pitted crews against one another in a competition to load the most tonnage during an eight-hour shift. This lowered safety standards even further, but it sped up the work and increased morale, so it was encouraged. Some officers placed bets on which crew could load the most tonnage in a shift. A local longshoremen's union and the U.S. Coast Guard offered advice on safer loading methods, but the officers in charge ignored it.

On the evening of July 17, two merchant ships, the S.S. *Quinault Victory* on its maiden voyage and the 440-foot S.S. *E. A. Bryan*, were docked at the loading pier, one on either side. The ships were bound for the Pacific Theater of Operations. The hold of the *E. A. Bryan* was almost

After the explosion, what little remained
of the S.S. *Quinault Victory* lay upside down in the bay.
PHOTOGRAPH FROM THE U.S. DEPARTMENT OF DEFENSE,
COURTESY OF THE NATIONAL PARK SERVICE.

filled with explosives, while the *Quinault Victory* was empty, awaiting its load. Another 4,600 tons of explosives were nearby on sixteen rail cars, including ammunition, bombs, and depth charges. Hundreds of men were working on or around the ships and pier when, at 10:18 P.M., a series of explosions ripped through the two ships and the pier. The *Bryan* and all the buildings near it were blown to bits. The *Quinault Victory* was spun into the air and broken in pieces, and the stern of the ship landed upside down in the bay about 500 feet away.

Witnesses a mile away reported hearing splintering wood as the first explosion split the night. They said there was a bright white flash and a sharp report, followed in a few seconds by a huge explosion. Sailors wondered if the Japanese were bombing them in a replay of Pearl Harbor. The blast blew out the windows in nearby barracks, cutting and blinding the men sleeping there. One man said it was so bright out for a moment that he thought the sun had come up. Others said that flashes in the sky

The explosion blew out windows at the Port Chicago
barracks and left parts of the building crumpled.
PHOTOGRAPH FROM THE U.S. DEPARTMENT OF DEFENSE,
COURTESY OF THE NATIONAL PARK SERVICE.

looked like fireworks on the Fourth of July. Then someone shouted that the barracks were collapsing, and everyone rushed out just before sections of the building crumbled.

Fiery chunks of metal came raining down all over the base. In downtown Port Chicago, customers were watching a war movie and thought the sounds they heard were simply part of the show—until a wall of the building buckled and the roof began to cave in. Some people in town were showered with splintered glass and flying debris. Every building in Port Chicago was damaged. Unexploded shells fell back to earth over a two-mile area. The blast crumpled walls and blew out windows in the nearby towns of Martinez and Pittsburg, and the Benecia Arsenal buildings almost four miles across Suisun Bay suffered considerable damage. Some damage even extended as far away as San Francisco, where it was reported that windows blew out in the St. Francis Hotel.

A truck arrived at the barracks and took a load of men down to the pier. But when they arrived, they found there was no pier, no locomotive, no boxcars, and no ships, either. Everything had been blown away. Men arriving at the scene extinguished flames near a remaining boxcar of munitions before it could detonate. Others began ferrying the injured to nearby hospitals.

The blast instantly killed 320 people. It was the greatest loss of life on the American home front of the entire war. Of those killed, 202 were African Americans, enlisted Navy personnel who were working as loaders, and 9 were naval officers supervising them. Sixty-four men were crewmen on the *E. A. Bryan* and the *Quinault Victory*. Also killed were thirty-three members of the U.S. Navy Armed Guard who were attached to the two cargo ships. Three civilian Navy employees and three civilian contractors

Pier 1 was reduced to a pile of debris.
PHOTOGRAPH FROM THE U.S. DEPARTMENT OF DEFENSE,
COURTESY OF THE NATIONAL PARK SERVICE.

lost their lives, as did a Marine guard and the five-man crew of a U.S. Coast Guard fire boat. In addition to the dead, 390 people were injured.

The explosions created a seismic shock felt as far away as Nevada. Seismologists later reported that the blast registered 3.5 on the Richter scale. Investigators later discovered a blast crater under where the ships had been moored that was 60 feet deep, 300 feet wide, and 700 feet long.

Within a few days of the explosions, the commandant of the Twelfth Naval District, Admiral Carleton H. Wright, issued a press statement: "As was to be expected, Negro personnel . . . performed bravely and efficiently in the emergency. . . . As real Navy men, they simply carried on in the crisis . . . in accordance with our Service's highest traditions." A memorial service for the victims of the explosions was held on July 30, 1944, at Port Chicago. Navy planes scattered flowers on the water. The remains of forty of the victims were interred at Golden Gate National Cemetery.

Congress began working on a bill to compensate residents of Port Chicago and the families of the servicemen who were killed. The initial proposal was for up to $5,000 for each sailor lost, but on learning that most of the money would be paid to African Americans, Representative John Rankin of Mississippi succeeded in lowering the top compensation amount to $3,000.

The exact cause of the explosions was never determined. A Navy court of inquiry blamed officers at the facility for lax safety standards but suggested that the disaster was sparked by rough handling of the explosives by personnel. Ignoring the Navy's culpability for the lack of training provided to the men—and voicing the racism of the era—the court concluded that "the colored enlisted personnel are neither temperamentally or intellectually capable of handling high explosives."

About two-thirds of those killed in the Port Chicago explosion were African-American Navy personnel. The surviving men in these units—those who had helped put out the fire and rescue the injured—were sent to the nearby Mare Island facility. Unlike the officers at Port Chicago, who had been given a month's leave, the enlisted men were given no leave. They received no additional training, but within a month they were again assigned to loading explosives onto ships. Initially, 328 of the men refused to handle explosives again. When individually ordered to do so, 70 finally gave in.

The remaining 258 who refused were put under guard and loaded onto a prison barge. A few days later, Admiral Wright addressed the men and told them that their failure to follow orders in a time of war amounted to mutiny, for which they could be shot. The threat of a firing squad was enough to scare 208 of the sailors back to work. They were tried by summary court-martial on the charge of refusing to obey orders and sentenced to a loss of three months' pay.

Fifty men held out. They were first imprisoned at Camp Shoemaker near Dublin, California, and later at Treasure Island, a naval installation in the bay between San Francisco and Oakland, where they were to be court-martialed. The prisoners were questioned during August and formally charged with mutiny in September. This was the largest such trial in U.S. Navy history. The prosecutor was Lieutenant Commander James F. Coakley, formerly the assistant district attorney of nearby Alameda County. The hearings lasted six weeks.

The case caught the attention of Thurgood Marshall, who would later be appointed to the U.S. Supreme Court but who, at the time, was chief counsel for the National Association for the Advancement of Colored People, or NAACP. Marshall sat in for the last few days of the proceedings. He later argued, "This is not 50 men on trial for mutiny. This is the Navy on trial for its whole vicious policy towards Negroes." Despite the protests of Marshall and others, the Navy trial board deliberated for only eighty minutes before finding the fifty black sailors guilty on October 24, 1944. They were sentenced to prison terms that ranged from eight to fifteen years of hard labor, were reduced in rank to apprentice seamen, and were to be dishonorably discharged after completing their prison terms.

In November, the men were moved to the Naval Disciplinary Barracks at Terminal Island near Long Beach, where long-term prisoners were housed.

Thurgood Marshall went to work immediately to mount an appeal. In April 1945, he went to the office of the Navy Judge Advocate General to present evidence that the men's actions did not constitute a mutiny and that they had been made scapegoats for the disaster. His appeal was denied. Letters protesting the sentences of the fifty men poured in, including one from former first lady Eleanor Roosevelt, who appealed on behalf of the convicted men to Secretary of the Navy James Forrestal. She sent him a persuasive NAACP pamphlet along with a handwritten note that read, "I hope in the case of these boys special care will be taken."

All the attention focused on the case forced the Navy to strengthen safety procedures for loading munitions, provide better training for those handling the loading, and modify the munitions themselves to make them safer to load. The Navy began to use integrated crews—white and African-American sailors—to load munitions. The Navy also reevaluated the punishment it had meted out to the men at Port Chicago, and after sixteen months behind bars almost all of the men were released to regular duty and later discharged "under honorable conditions." A month later, in February 1946, the Navy became the first branch of the U.S. military to fully desegregate its ranks. But the wheels of justice grind slowly. In the 1990s, efforts to exonerate the fifty African-American seamen mostly failed but did lead President Bill Clinton to pardon Freddie Meeks, one of the few members of the Port Chicago fifty who were still alive at the time. Meeks died in 2003.

A bill to create a Port Chicago Naval Magazine National Memorial, originally sponsored by Congressman George Miller from California, was

Today, the disaster site is dedicated as the Port Chicago Naval Magazine National Memorial, administered by the National Park Service.
PHOTOGRAPH BY LUTHER BAILEY, COURTESY OF THE NATIONAL PARK SERVICE.

signed into law by President Barack Obama in October 2009. It designated the memorial and five acres of land that encompass the Port Chicago explosions as an official part of the National Park Service, enabling the agency to allocate funds for the upkeep and preservation of the park and for education about its importance.

SOURCES

Paddle Wheeler Explosions

Garvey, Stan. *King and Queen of the River: The Legendary Paddle-Wheel Steamboats Delta King and Delta Queen*. River Heritage Press, 1995.

MacMullen, Jerry. *Paddle-wheel Days in California*. Stanford University, CA: Stanford University Press, 1944.

Nolte, Carl. "Jenny Lind ferry disaster commemoration." *San Francisco Chronicle*. April 12, 2013.

Nolte, Carl. "The tragedy of the Jenny Lind steamboat." SFGate. April 13, 2013.

"Sacramento History/The Steamboat." Trips into History. January 25, 2013.

Schell, Hall. "When Paddlewheeler Steamboats Sloshed through Delta Waterways." California Delta Chambers. October 30, 1998.

Secrest, William B., Jr. and William B. Secrest, Sr. *California Disasters, 1812–1899*. Quill Driver Books/Word Dancer Press, 2006.

The Wreck of the *Brother Jonathan*

Associated Press. "Agreement on Treasure of Lost Ship is Ratified." *The New York Times*. March 14, 1999.

Belyk, Robert C. *Great Shipwrecks of the Pacific Coast*. New York, NY: John Wiley & Sons, 2001.

Manson, Bill. "Courtroom Treasure Hunters." *San Diego Reader*. January 8, 1998.

Powers, Dennis M. *Sentinel of the Seas: Life and Death at the Most Dangerous Lighthouse Ever Built*. New York, NY: Citadel Press, 2007.

Powers, Dennis M. *Treasure Ship: The Legend and Legacy of the S. S. Brother Jonathan*. New York, NY: Citadel Press, 2006.

Secrest, William B., Jr. and William B. Secrest, Sr. *California Disasters, 1812–1899.* Sanger, CA: Quill Driver Books/Word Dancer Press, Inc., 2006.

Wheeler, Wayne. "St. George Reef: America's Most Expensive Lighthouse." *The Keeper's Log.* Fall 1985.

Wiltsee, Ernest A. *Gold Rush Steamers of the Pacific.* Lawrence, MA: Quarterman Publications, 1976.

Port Chicago Munitions Explosions

Allen, Robert L. *The Port Chicago Mutiny.* New York, NY: Amistad Press, 1989.

Andrews, Evan. "Port Chicago Disaster Stuns the Nation, 70 Years Ago." History. July 17, 2014.

Madrigal, Alexis. "The Port Chicago Explosion (1944)." Oakland Museum of California.

Port Chicago Naval Magazine Explosion, 1944. Naval History and Heritage Command. November 20, 2017.

Port Chicago Naval Magazine National Memorial. National Park Service. U.S. Department of the Interior, Martinez, California, 2011.

Sheinkin, Steve. *The Port Chicago 50: Disaster, Mutiny, and the Fight for Civil Rights.* New York, NY: Roaring Brook Press, 2015.

This Day in History. "An ammunition ship explodes in the Port Chicago disaster." November 13, 2009.

FLOODS AND A TSUNAMI

CALIFORNIA PERIODICALLY EXPERIENCES ONSLAUGHTS OF PRECIPitation streaming in from the Pacific Ocean that fill lakes and rivers and inundate low-lying areas. Scientists say the geologic record and other evidence indicates that widespread flooding is a normal aspect of the region's climate and topography dating back to prehistoric times.

In the modern era, two flood years stand out as among the worst—1862 and 2017—and there are parallels in their stories. California also experienced the worst tsunami to strike the mainland United States, in 1964.

THE GREAT FLOOD OF 1862

On January 10, 1862, the governor-elect of the state of California was making his way to the capitol in Sacramento for his inauguration. There was no cheering crowd lining the street. In fact, no street was visible at all. Leland Stanford was riding to his ceremony in a rowboat. The Great Flood of 1862 was in full spate.

Sacramento was under ten feet of water, and it was still rising at the rate of one foot an hour. Frantic residents were trying to flee the city.

Water filled the streets of Sacramento
during the Great Flood of 1862.
PHOTOGRAPH COURTESY OF THE CALIFORNIA
DEPARTMENT OF WATER RESOURCES.

The inauguration ceremony was kept as short as possible, after which Stanford was rowed back to his mansion. There, the floodwaters were so deep, he was forced to enter his home through a second-story window.

The Great Flood of 1862 was the largest that settlers had ever seen in California, Oregon, and the Territory of Nevada. William H. Brewer, a geology professor working with the Whitmore Geological Society, wrote from San Francisco on January 19, 1862, "The amount of rain that has fallen is unprecedented in the history of this state." At a 1996 symposium on California rainfall and floods, James Goodridge, the state climatologist, classified the 1862 flood as "an historic 1,000-year storm." It was both rare and dreadful.

California had undergone many floods, but no one alive in 1862 had seen such widespread floodwaters. The flood created a lake in the middle of the state that was 300 miles long and 20 miles wide. It was similar in size and shape to Lake Superior. This flood began in December 1861 and lasted through January 1862. Parts of Northern California remained un-livable until the summer of that year.

When rain began around November 10, farmers were grateful. It had been dry, and people were happy at first to finally see the moisture. On October 4, 1861, the *Red Bluff Independent* reported, "Six months have elapsed since rain has fallen on Red Bluff. This has been the driest, hottest season since California became a state."

But the welcome rains didn't stop. They continued falling for four weeks with little intermission. A series of Arctic storms dropped ten to fifteen feet of snow in the Sierra Nevada, so there was a heavy snowpack. On December 8, a warm tropical storm reached Northern California. Such a storm is like an atmospheric river, a narrow band of water vapor that forms about a mile above the ocean and extends for miles. A newspaper in Grass Valley reported that nine inches of rain fell in thirty-six hours. This tropical storm not only dumped rain, but it melted the snowpack, sending water rushing down streams and rivers.

The swollen rivers wreaked havoc on settlements around the state. In the north, six miles from the mouth of the Klamath River, flooding washed away seventeen of the twenty buildings at Fort Ter-Waw on the Klamath River Reservation in Del Norte County. The damage was so severe that the fort was never rebuilt. The garrison was moved to Camp Lincoln in Crescent City. In Placer County, 45 Chinese miners drowned when a river washed away their settlement. Another report claimed that almost 1,000 Chinese were swept to their death from the vicinity of Long Bar on the Yuba River. Every day there were additional reports of drownings. Many of these victims had remained in their cabins during the rains, hoping to be safe there, but as waters rose, the cabins were swept away. The North Fork of the American River at Auburn rose thirty-five feet. Settlements all along rivers were destroyed. Parts of Marysville, Auburn, and Santa Rosa were underwater. Roads and bridges were washed out. The Feather River was reported to be nine feet higher than had ever been recorded before.

On December 23, a second tropical storm hit and lasted for four days. Some mining towns were completely submerged. On the Stanislaus River near Knight's Ferry, bridges and roads were wiped out and there was almost complete destruction over a forty-mile reach. Much of the Trinity River drainage was stripped bare of bridges.

Sacramento is located at the junction of the Sacramento and American Rivers. The valley there is a flat, forty-mile-wide plain. The original city was built only sixteen feet above low-water mark. After flooding in 1849, 1850, 1851, 1852, and 1853, dirt was brought in and layered onto the streets, raising the business district about four feet. A levee was built along the banks of the Sacramento and American Rivers in the hope of preventing future flooding. But the storms that came through during December 1861 and January 1862 dashed those hopes.

Between January 9 and 17, two more tropical storms hit, melting the Sierra snowpack and dumping rain. Water came rushing down into Sacramento from both the American and Sacramento Rivers. Buildings were destroyed and part of the city was beneath thirty feet of water. Governor Stanford and other elected officials moved out of the capitol in Sacramento and conducted the state's business from San Francisco. The clear blue waters of San Francisco Bay turned brown with muddy runoff.

The levee at the junction of the Sacramento and American Rivers acted like a dam during the storm, holding floodwaters in the city of Sacramento. Crews finally cut through the levee, reducing the water level in the city by about six feet. The flood greatly widened the Sacramento River. John Carr, a passenger who traveled on a steamer from Sacramento to Red Bluff during the flood, said that the only way the boat captain could find the riverbed was to look for the cottonwood trees that lined its banks. Carr noted that the steamer stopped several times to rescue people from trees and rooftops of houses that were now in the river.

The water was so deep in some places that it covered the telegraph poles that had just been installed to complete the line between New York and the West Coast. Communication was cut off for more than a month. Mail could not be delivered because roads and bridges were underwater or had washed away. People in two-story houses in Sacramento tried to live upstairs. But houses made of wood were often lifted off their foundations by the floods and floated away. In some cases, boats were sent to rescue people from their floating homes. Elsewhere, farm houses, cattle, sheep, and household furniture and possessions were all washed away and lost in the raging floodwaters.

In Stockton, floodwaters took out part of the town square, broke away bridges and causeways, and continued rushing southward. Many people were without homes, spare clothing, or any provisions.

The flood didn't just affect the northern half of the state. Sixty-six inches of rain fell in Los Angeles, four times the area's usual average annual rainfall. Rivers overflowed their banks, causing muddy lakes to form in normally arid areas, including in the Mojave Desert. The Santa Ana River flooded near Anaheim, creating an inland lake four feet deep and four miles long that remained for four months. In the San Gabriel Mountains, the tiny mining town of Eldoradoville was swept away. Fruit trees and vineyards were destroyed all along the Los Angeles River. In San Bernardino County, churches rang their bells to alert residents, saving the people of Agua Mansa on the banks of the Santa Ana River, where floodwaters swept away all but the church and one home. (Ironically, *agua mansa* translates as "gentle water.") The town was never rebuilt, and today all that remains is the Agua Mansa Pioneer Cemetery southwest of the Interstate 10 and 215 interchange in Colton. In San Diego at the time of the flood, there was also a storm at sea that backed up the floodwaters and created a new river channel into San Diego Bay.

The storms and flooding of 1862 affected a wide swath of the West beyond California. For example, in Oregon, Linn City, Champoeg, and Orleans were destroyed and never rebuilt. Flour mills and grain storage facilities, often located close to a river's edge, were damaged or destroyed. Homes, farms, and businesses along rivers such as the Willamette, Umpqua, Coquille, and Rogue suffered heavy damage. At the same time, similar flooding caused damage in Nevada, Utah, and Arizona as heavy rains swelled their rivers to overflowing.

The costs of the widespread flooding were enormous, and thousands of lives were lost. An accurate count is simply not available. In addition, California lost about one-quarter of its taxable property. The state came close to declaring bankruptcy. One in eight homes was washed away or totally destroyed. An estimated one-quarter of the state's 800,000 cattle drowned. More than 600,000 sheep and lambs died in the flood. Trees were uprooted and acres of forests destroyed. Fruit trees were swept away. Mining and lumbering equipment was lost. Damage, loss, and devastation were felt in countless ways. In Oakland, the fresh water and silt rushing into San Francisco Bay destroyed many of the oyster beds.

Also lost was a sense of optimism. Could flooding be controlled and did California have a future? The answer required rebuilding and decades of engineering new dams, catchments, levees, and other water-management structures. And yet the same weather phenomena—atmospheric rivers such as the Pineapple Express—continue to periodically bring catastrophic flooding to California's fertile valleys.

FLOODS OF 2017

After years of devastating drought, California was more than ready for rain, but not in the huge quantities that arrived at the end of 2016 and beginning of 2017. That winter was the wettest in a century of record keeping. Almost ninety inches of precipitation fell in the Sierra Nevada between October 2016 and April 2017, and those mountains supply a large amount of California's water.

In early January 2017, some peaks in the Sierra Nevada received twelve feet of snow in a week. The precipitation arrived via a weather system called the Pineapple Express, which is an "atmospheric river," a narrow strip of concentrated moisture in the upper atmosphere. These systems originate around Hawaii and collect large amounts of moisture from the Pacific Ocean.

The wave of storms knocked out power for 570,000 Northern California customers. The Russian River in Sonoma County rose three feet above flood level. As the river overflowed its banks, it forced the overnight evacuation of more than 3,000 residents in Guerneville, west of Santa Rosa.

East of Sacramento, the American River reached record levels, but Folsom Dam contained the excess flow, averting widespread flooding. South of San Francisco in Monterey County, twenty-seven homes were damaged when the Carmel River overflowed and swamped the town of Seaside.

On January 23, the National Weather Service reported that a wave in Monterey Bay reached a height of 34.12 feet, a record for the bay. Monster waves destroyed the remains of the *Palo Alto*, a World War I–era ship moored in Aptos. Its stern was connected to a pier at Seaside State Beach. Built in 1919 as a tanker, too late for use in the war, it was later stripped and refurbished. A ballroom was added, where famous orchestras led by Benny Goodman and Tommy Dorsey played. It was a well-known tourist attraction often referred to as "the cement ship."

On January 22, Southern California was hit with a third wave of rainstorms. A flash flood warning was in effect for much of the area. Especially hard hit was Long Beach, where intersections were flooded and parked cars inundated. In some neighborhoods, the water was so deep that motorists had to be rescued. Several teens attempted to raft the Los Angeles River, but they had to be rescued and taken to a hospital. On Interstate 5, in the Grapevine area near Lebec, sleet and hail caused a fifteen-car collision, injuring nine people. In Los Angeles, crews responded to 172 weather-related incidents, including flooding, fires, and fallen trees.

In Pomona, a motorist lost control of a car in heavy rain, crashed into a telephone pole, and was killed. As rains continued to pound the California coast, a cliff and patio collapsed into the ocean at Isla Vista in Santa Barbara County. Fifteen to twenty residents were evacuated from their oceanfront units. Rockslides closed down Topanga Canyon Boulevard in Malibu.

As Californians throughout the state tried to deal with torrential rains, debris slides, potential dam failures, road closures, and flooded homes, some managed to keep a sense of humor. One man from Carpinteria on the coast told the Associated Press in a Facebook message, "At one point the wind was so strong I'm surprised it didn't blow my windows out. I now have a pond in my patio. And my dog is starting to grow flippers, so he can go out and do his business."

By February 2017, high runoff was creating a crisis at the Oroville Dam in Butte County, north of Sacramento. Completed in 1968, the dam is 770 feet tall; it's the tallest dam in the United States and the highest earthen embankment dam in the world. It impounds Lake Oroville, which is the second-largest man-made lake in California. The reservoir is used for flood control, water storage, and hydroelectric power generation.

On February 7, 2017, dam operators opened the main concrete spillway of the dam to compensate for high inflows to the reservoir. But they noticed a strange spill pattern and shut off the flow of water over the spillway. An inspection revealed a crater in the half-mile-long concrete chute. Two more test releases enlarged the spillway crater even more. The dam managers had to decide whether to continue to use the main spillway, knowing it could be further damaged, or allow the lake to flow over an untested emergency spillway. This spillway consisted of a concrete weir, or wall, at the top of an unpaved hillside. It was intended to serve as a last resort. Because it was unpaved, the water would run uncontrolled down the hillside. The dam operators decided to continue to use the main spillway but to reduce the flow of water over it. They announced that there was no danger to the public.

But the lake kept rising, and on February 11 water poured over the emergency spillway and down the earthen hillside for the first time. Within a day, engineers discovered that this was causing erosion and threatening to undercut the concrete at the top of the spillway. Engineers worried that this could collapse the wall at the top of the dam and send billions of tons of water down the Feather River toward the city of Oroville, just five miles downstream. Officials ordered a mandatory evacuation for 188,000 people along the Feather River in Butte, Yuba, and Sutter Counties. Some were given thirty minutes to gather their things; others were told to leave immediately.

To reduce erosion below the auxiliary spillway, dam operators released
more water down the damaged main spillway at Oroville Dam.
PHOTOGRAPH BY WILLIAM CROYLE, CALIFORNIA DEPARTMENT OF WATER RESOURCES.

When dam operators were finally able to stop releasing water
down the main spillway, the scope of damage became apparent.
PHOTOGRAPH COURTESY OF CALIFORNIA DEPARTMENT OF WATER RESOURCES.

To reduce the pressure on the emergency spillway, dam operators increased the flow of water over the main spillway. By 9 P.M. on February 12, the level of the lake had dropped, and water stopped flowing over the emergency spillway. Engineers immediately began shoring up the eroded hillside, using helicopters to drop rocks and sandbags onto the eroded area. Also, 28,000 members of the National Guard were placed on standby for deployment if the spillway failed. But the dam held and, on February 14, evacuees were allowed to return to their homes. A huge disaster had been averted, but the cost of repairs to the dam was estimated at $1.1 billion.

With all the heavy runoff, water managers opened the Sacramento Weir for the first time since 2006, diverting floodwaters away from Sacramento and instead filling a floodway known as the Yolo Bypass. This floodway is three miles wide and forty-one miles long; full of water, it looked like an inland sea.

More than 100 residents of Maxwell (population 1,100), near Interstate 5 in Colusa County, had to be rescued by boats when flash flooding hit Stone Corral Creek. In Mono County, U.S. Highway 395 was temporarily closed in both directions. In Santa Clara County, Anderson Dam overflowed for the first time in eleven years. The reservoir reached full capacity

Floodwaters flow through the Sacramento Weir into the Yolo Bypass on January 10, 2017.
PHOTOGRAPH COURTESY OF THE CALIFORNIA DEPARTMENT OF WATER RESOURCES.

and began cascading over the spillway; the adjacent town of Morgan Hill found itself with a spectacular waterfall. The spillway at Anderson Dam was fine, but there was still worry. The reservoir was normally kept at only 68 percent capacity because the dam wasn't seismically stable, meaning an earthquake could damage it and send a wall of water into Morgan Hill and nearby San Jose. In an effort to keep the water level down, the water district released water from Anderson Reservoir through an opening at the bottom of the lake. But the heavy rains added water to the reservoir at a faster rate than it could be released.

As a series of heavy downpours hit between February 17 and 22, flooding increased. Mandatory evacuation was ordered for 1,400 residents in San Jose along Coyote Creek, which flows from Anderson Reservoir and was rising dangerously. Flood stage was 10 feet, and the water rose to 14.4 feet. Nineteen roads were closed. In some cases, boats were used to rescue residents. Both San Jose and San Francisco broke historical daily rainfall records.

In Central California, the San Joaquin River reached record highs as water was released from upriver dams. On February 20, a levee breached at Manteca, and 500 people had to be evacuated. The famous Pioneer Cabin Tree, a giant sequoia in Calaveras Big Trees State Park and a favorite of countless visitors who had passed through it, collapsed. Near Big Sur, a section of the Pacific Coast Highway was closed due to bridge collapses and mudslides. The San Francisco International Airport recorded a new one-day record amount of daily rainfall on February 20. An area known as Three Peaks in Monterey County on the Los Padres National Forest received 8.03 inches of rain in 204 minutes.

In Southern California, the storms of February 16–19 claimed the lives of five people who drowned in the Greater Los Angeles area. Many highways were closed due to flooding. Water 2.5 feet deep swamped Interstate 5 in Sun Valley and trapped several motorists. In Santa Barbara, muddy debris slides from hillsides that had burned during the 2011–2017 drought years closed U.S. Highway 101, and the town of Goleta was evacuated.

Tens of thousands of people in Southern California were left without power. Flash flood warnings were issued for Orange County and parts of San Diego. One man in Sherman Oaks in Los Angeles was electrocuted when he stepped into water that was charged by a live power line knocked down by a falling tree. Another person was found dead in a submerged car in Victorville, and two fatal accidents on a San Diego interstate were attributed to heavy rain. Police in Ventura County reported another death when a man in his car was swept by the water into a gully.

In Studio City, two cars drove into a sinkhole that opened up in the road. The driver of one car was able to get out on his own. The woman in the second car was rescued when the fire department lowered a ladder ten feet to help her climb to safety.

After the fierce series of rains in January and February of 2017 finally ended, Californians began to clean up and repair roads, bridges, and entire towns. The state's long drought was over, and many lakes and reservoirs throughout the state were full again. New Melonas Lake, which was only one-quarter full in 2016, reached 90 percent capacity in June 2017. Lake Berryessa in Napa County filled for the first time since 2006, while Lake Isabella in Kern County reached capacity for the first time in six years. Lake Tahoe received the most precipitation it had seen in 117 years.

CRESCENT CITY TSUNAMI, 1964

Crescent City is perched along the northern coast of California about twenty miles south of the Oregon border. It's named for the long, crescent-shaped beach that stretches south of town. Between the beach and downtown lies the city's harbor, bookended by two jetties. Unfortunately, these features and the topography of the nearby sea floor tend to funnel tsunamis toward the harbor and downtown. The town is accustomed to waves surging ashore; since 1933, thirty-one tsunamis have hit Crescent City. Most of them were small or even imperceptible, but at least four tsunamis here caused damage, including one that was the most destructive to hit the West Coast to date.

Today, Crescent City is bedecked with tsunami-zone warning signs and route markers leading to higher ground. Residents and visitors alike can't help but be aware of the risk and of the appropriate response if the tsunami sirens go off—drop whatever you're doing and immediately head to higher ground. Decades ago, however, the locals were a bit more relaxed about their town's occasional high-water problem.

When a tsunami struck on the night of March 27, 1964, the first wave partially flooded downtown. Gary Clawson and his father, Bill, who owned the Long Branch Tavern, weren't overly concerned. The two men, along with Gary's mother, his fiancée, a friend, and two employees, went to the tavern to check on the damage, empty the cash register, and have a drink to celebrate Bill's birthday.

No sooner had they downed the birthday drink than the next wave of the tsunami hit. Water came rushing in the back door of the tavern. Everyone climbed up on tables and chairs, but soon only their heads were above water as the building continued to flood. The water eventually lifted the Long Branch off its foundation. The Clawsons and their friends and employees barely escaped onto the tavern roof as the building began to float in the surging waters. Gary Clawson made it to dry land, got a boat, rowed out, and picked up his family and friends. Then, as he rowed them toward land, the water quickly receded and pulled them back toward the bay. One friend escaped by catching hold of a bridge as they passed under it. The boat capsized, and everyone still aboard drowned except Gary Clawson, who with difficulty swam to safety. In all, eleven people died that night in Crescent City due to the tsunami.

But this tragic tale actually starts in Alaska. March 27, 1964, was Good Friday, but it became a day of tragedy when at 5:36 P.M. local time an enormous earthquake struck near Prince William Sound, about eighty miles southeast of Anchorage. The magnitude 9.2 quake was the strongest ever to strike North America and the second-strongest earthquake ever recorded worldwide. The shaking lasted for about four and a half minutes as 600 miles of fault ruptured at once, permanently lifting the ground in some areas by as much as thirty-eight feet.

The earthquake caused widespread damage in Alaska at Whittier, Seward, and Kodiak. Valdez was leveled. A chasm opened up beneath the S.S. *Chena*, the first supply ship to arrive after the spring thaw; it had just docked at Valdez. The quake and subsequent tsunami tossed the 441-foot freighter like a toy, nearly swallowed it in a whirlpool, and then slammed it down where the dock, now destroyed, had been.

In Anchorage, buildings collapsed, power lines toppled, roads fractured, and cars were destroyed. Massive landslides demolished entire neighborhoods. As coastal lands and the seabed rose and fell, the shifting displaced billions of tons of ocean water and set off a tremendous tsunami.

A tsunami's speed is dependent on the depth of the water; it moves faster in deeper water. This particular tsunami traveled throughout the Pacific Ocean, reaching Japan within six hours, Australia within fourteen hours, and even Antarctica in twenty-one hours. The main wave achieved heights of 150 feet in open water, and within just a few hours it steamrolled ashore along the coasts of southeast Alaska, British Columbia, Washington, Oregon, and California.

The 9.2 earthquake near Anchorage that generated
the tsunami caused massive damage in Alaska.
PHOTOGRAPH COURTESY OF THE NATIONAL OCEANIC AND ATMOSPHERIC ADMINISTRATION.

Several towns on the west coast of Vancouver Island were hit hard. Port Alberni sits at the head of a long, narrow fjord that funneled the surge in two waves, destroying 55 homes and damaging another 375. Overall, damage in British Columbia was estimated at $75 million in today's U.S. dollars.

Heading south faster than a passenger jet, the tsunami caused millions of dollars of damage in Washington and Oregon. In Washington, a grandmother hearing about the impending tsunami was worried about her granddaughter, who was camping at Kalaloch Beach on the Olympic Peninsula. She phoned her daughter, who rushed to the beach, arriving just five minutes ahead of the wave. The daughter and granddaughter ran to higher ground and survived but were in water up to their knees. Fishing boats and nets were damaged, and highways, bridges, and homes were destroyed or damaged all along the Washington coast.

In Seaside, Oregon, several homes were badly damaged, one bridge and railroad trestle were destroyed, and other roads and bridges were damaged. Some of this damage occurred inland as water surged up creek channels.

The tsunami brought tragedy to Beverly Beach State Park just north of Newport, Oregon. There, Monte and Rita McKenzie were camped in a driftwood shelter on the beach with their four children, Louise, Bobby, Ricky, and Tammy. The children, all between the ages of three and eight, were in their sleeping bags. When the first wave surged ashore, the parents frantically clutched their children, but then the bigger waves hit, separating the family in the dark. All four children and the family dog were swept away and drowned; only Ricky's body was recovered.

Of all these far-flung locales, the tsunami hit Crescent City the hardest. This small fishing and lumber town more than 1,500 miles from Anchorage was home to about 3,000 residents in 1964. The Sea Wave Warning System in Honolulu issued a tsunami advisory bulletin at 9:30 P.M. Experts estimated that the first wave would hit Crescent City about midnight, but there was nothing to suggest the size of the expected waves. The first wave of the tsunami struck at 11:39 P.M. local time and came inland two blocks, flooding the lower half of town to Second Street.

Battery Point Lighthouse, just west of Crescent City Harbor, withstood the tsunami.
PHOTOGRAPH BY FRANK SCHULENBURG, CC BY-SA 3.0.

After this, people thought the worst was over, as had typically been the case with other smaller tsunamis that had struck the town. Most people were unaware that large tsunamis typically come in multiple waves and that the crests of these waves can come several hours apart. Often, the first wave in the series is not the strongest. Police tried to keep general sightseers away as they came for a closer look at the damage they were hearing about on radio and television, but local residents and business owners were allowed downtown. These people were hit by the second, third, and fourth waves, which they weren't expecting. The largest wave was nearly twenty-one feet tall as it surged toward town.

Clarence "Roxey" Coons and his wife, Peggy, were the keepers at the Battery Point Lighthouse, a fixture from the 1850s that stands on a tiny islet just 100 yards offshore from Crescent City. Peggy recalled that she woke and saw a full moon reflected in the sea, but something didn't look right. She roused her husband and they ventured outside to marvel at what they thought was a high tide filling the nearby harbor. As the water suddenly receded, they turned to face the ocean. Peggy later described the scene, documented in *The Raging Sea*, by Dennis Powers:

The basin was sucked dry. . . . In the distance, a black wall of water was rapidly building up, evidenced by a flash of white as the edge of the boiling and seething seawater reflected the moonlight.

Then the mammoth wall of water came barreling towards us. It was a terrifying mass, stretching up from the ocean floor and looking much higher than the island. Roxey shouted, "Let's head for the tower!"—but it was too late. "Look out!" he yelled, and we both ducked as the water struck, split and swirled over both sides of the island. It struck with such force and speed that we felt we were being carried along with the ocean. It took several minutes before we realized that the island hadn't moved.

When the tsunami assaulted the shore, it was like a violent explosion. A thunderous roar mingled with all the confusion. Everywhere we looked, buildings, cars, lumber, and boats shifted around like crazy. The whole beachfront moved, changing before our very eyes.

The century-old lighthouse—and the Coonses—survived the tsunami, but the situation in Crescent City had gone from bad to worse. As more water came rushing in, many people found themselves wading or swimming for their lives. Some were trapped in floating cars or desperately holding on to floating debris. Others were trapped on roofs. Rescuers used road graders and other heavy equipment to save some of these people.

One elderly woman was asleep in bed when the tsunami hit. She was unaware of what was going on until the roof of her house collapsed, pinning her in bed. Her house traveled three blocks in the floodwaters, and it was ten thirty the next morning before she was rescued after a passerby heard her cries for help.

The manager of a car-repair shop was only mildly concerned about flooding after the first wave hit. He called the shop owner, who arrived with his wife to check the damage. Then the second wave hit. The quick-thinking manager put the owner's car on the service rack and raised it to the top with the three of them in it. The shop filled with eight feet of water, and, although the car wobbled as water surged, the rack held and they survived.

As the tsunami rushed into downtown Crescent City, a fire broke out at the Pontiac Automobile Agency because of a shorted fuse box. Flames spread to nearby Texaco and Union Oil bulk tanks, which set off explosions adding to the chaos. The fire burned for several days.

Houses at the lower end of town were lifted from their foundations and began to float away. Although later reports gave differing accounts, it seems the second wave of the tsunami was smaller and barely noticed, while the third and fourth waves did the most damage. After the third wave, the drawdown was exceptional. Roxey Coon later estimated that the water receded three-quarters of a mile beyond the outer breakwater. The fourth wave, which peaked at about 2 A.M., was about 15.7 feet above the expected tide level.

The third and fourth waves were so high and so strong that they picked up logs, cars, and trucks and threw them against buildings like battering rams. The water stacked cars atop one another and even on rooftops. One big log battered its way right into the U.S. Post Office. The mail was sucked out, though much of it was later recovered. Downed electrical wires also posed serious hazards.

Harbor facilities were destroyed, and there was severe damage to twenty-nine blocks of town, including 172 businesses, 91 homes, and 12 house trailers. About twenty-one boats were sunk. Other boats—including the U.S. Coast Guard ninety-five-foot cutter *Cape Carter*, a logging tugboat, and several other fishing boats—survived by going out to the open ocean.

After the storm, debris was everywhere. As people cleaned, they found lots of dead fish, some in the most unlikely places, including residential flower boxes and even desk drawers. Total monetary value of damages in Crescent City was $7.5 million in 1964 dollars.

Tragically, at least eleven people drowned (including all but one of the Long Branch birthday party), twelve were hospitalized, and twelve received outpatient care. Many more had minor injuries. Besides Bill and Agatha Clawson, the dead included Adolph Arrigone, Jim Parks, Joan Fields, Lavella Hillsberry, Earl and Juanita Edwards, Donald McClure, and children Bonita and William Wright, who were just three years old and three months old, respectively.

South of Crescent City, most of the additional $1.5 million loss in California was to commercial fishing vessels, pleasure boats, and their docking facilities. At San Rafael, the tsunami picked up a dock with thirty boats anchored to it, lifted it over a levee, and deposited it about a quarter of a mile away. Several of the boats sank.

Many harbors were filled with silt and sand. In Sausalito, an older ferryboat that was being used as a store was torn from its moorings. The ferry and several pilings from the dock went sailing out into the bay. Considerable damage was done at Sausalito's Clipper Yacht Harbor. Marin County suffered more than $1 million in damage. At Half Moon Bay, some boats were sunk or swept out to sea and some ended up beached on rocks, but damage wasn't considered severe. In Santa Cruz, the waves from the tsunami were eleven feet high, sinking a hydraulic dredge and a thirty-two-foot cabin cruiser. But the water fell short of covering the boardwalk along the amusement park there. In San Francisco and even as far south as Los Angeles, the rush of water damaged piers and pleasure boats.

The tsunami of 1964 was so strong that it was observed around the Pacific Ocean. On the beaches in Hawaii, the wave was fifteen feet. Surges of over three feet were detected in Mexico, Chile, and New Zealand.

The seabed and shape of Crescent Bay and the city's harbor combine to magnify the power of tsunamis such as the 1964 surge.
PHOTOGRAPH COURTESY OF THE U.S. ARMY CORPS OF ENGINEERS.

In 1965, the Crescent City Rotary Club erected a sculpture and plaque dedicated to the memory of local tsunami victims. The memorial is located in Tsunami Landing Plaza and features a bronze abstract designed by Bruno Groth featuring seagulls and fish in a pool with spraying water jets. A granite stone in the pool wall lists the names of those who were killed in the disaster.

Today, some people think of Crescent City as "Tsunami City, USA," because of the frequency with which tsunamis have reached the town. Experts point out that Crescent City gets so badly damaged because the harbor is small and waves tend to get trapped between the jetties and slosh around. This is true whether the tsunami comes from Alaska, Chile, or Japan. Many tsunamis have been small. Several have been large and damaging. But the tsunami following Alaska's Good Friday Earthquake of 1964 is etched in history as the big one—so far.

SOURCES

The Great Flood of 1862

Elliott, Wallace. *History of Fresno County, California*. San Francisco, CA: Elliott, Wallace, Pub., 1882.

Goodridge, Jim. "Data on California's Extreme Rainfall from 1862–1995," 1996 California Weather Symposium, "Theme: A Prehistoric Look at California Rainfall and Floods," Sierra College, Rocklin, California, June 29, 1996.

McLaughlin, Mark. "Comets, volcanic eruptions and 10 FEET of rainfall: 1861-1862, California's most devastating winter." *Tahoe Weekly*. April 3, 2017.

The New York Times. "The Great Flood in California; Great Destruction of Property." January 21, 1862.

Roberts, Robert B. "Historic California Posts, Camps, Stations and Airfields: Fort Ter-Waw." Fortwiki, February 8, 2016.

Severson, Thor. *Sacramento: An illustrated History: 1839 to 1874 from Sutter's Fort to Capital City*. Sacramento, CA: California Historical Society, 1973.

Floods of 2017

Davies, Richard. "More Record Rain in California, 1000s Evacuate Floods in San Jose." *Floodlist*. February 22, 2017.

Department of Water Resources. *Oroville Dam: Key Unit of the State Water Project*. The Resources Agency, State of California. August 5, 1964.

Flood Control Infrastructure: Safety Questions Raised by Current Event. Hearing Before the Committee on Environment and Public Works, United States Senate. One hundred fifteenth Congress, first session. Washington, D.C.: U.S. Government Publishing Office, 2017.

Helsel, Phil and Chelsea Bailey. "Storm Socks Southern California, Flooding Freeways and Killing at Least 5." NBC News. February 17, 2017.

KPCC staff. "3rd California storm brings flooding, rockslides." KPCC News. January 23, 2017.

McQuillan, Lawrence. "The California Department of Water Resources Wins Dishonor of California Golden Fleece Award for its 'Patch and Pray' Approach to Dam Safety." Independent Institute. October 17, 2017.

Parvini, Sarah. "Northern California gets its wettest winter in nearly a century." *Los Angeles Times*. April 23, 2017.

Serna, Joseph. "Flooding, stranded livestock, and at least 4 dead as storms hit Northern California: 'They can't handle any more.'" *Los Angeles Times*. January 12, 2017.

Crescent City Tsunami, 1964

"1964 Alaska Earthquake." *History*. March 6, 2018.

Dougherty, Terri. *The Worst Tsunamis of All Time*. North Mankato, MN: Capstone Press, 2013.

Gonzales, Richard. "California Town Still Scarred by 1964 Tsunami." *Morning Edition*, National Public Radio. November 17, 2005.

Jones, Ray and Joe Lubow. *Disasters and Heroic Rescues of California*. Guilford, CT: Globe Pequot Press, 2006.

National Oceanic and Atmospheric Administration. "Tsunami Historical Series: Alaska—1964." *Science on a Sphere*.

Pararas-Carayannis, Dr. George. "The Effects of the March 27, 1964, Alaska Tsunami in California." *The Tsunami Page*. 2007.

Powers, Dennis. *The Raging Sea: The Powerful Account of the Worst Tsunami in U.S. History*. Sea Ventures Press, 2005.

Pratt, Sara E. "Benchmarks: March 27, 1964: The Good Friday Alaska Earthquake and Tsunamis." *Earth*. February 27, 2014.

Tsunamis Affecting the West Coast of the United States, 1806-1992. U.S. National Oceanic and Atmospheric Administration, National Environmental Satellite, Data, and Information Service, National Geophysical Data Center, Boulder, CO. 1993.

Wilson, Basil W. and Alf Torum. *TSUNAMI of the Alaskan Earthquake, 1964: Engineering Evaluation*. Washington, D.C.: U.S. Army Coastal Engineering Research Center, 1968.

AVALANCHES AND MUDSLIDES

IN SUFFICIENT QUANTITY, RAIN AND SNOW CAN CAUSE OR CONTRIBUTE to untold misery—see Chapter 2 on the Donner Party and Chapter 4 on floods. But blend precipitation with slope and gravity, and you have a recipe for unleashing a terrible, if localized, destructive power.

Unfortunately, California is well situated for avalanches and mudslides. Prevailing winds regularly deliver copious amounts of moisture, and then the state's steep, towering mountain ranges rake that moisture from the clouds. When enough rain percolates into soils or snow piles deep on those mountain slopes, gravity—and perhaps a triggering event—does the rest. The tales in this chapter reveal the risks of living on the steeps.

SNOW AND ROCK AVALANCHES STRIKE MONO COUNTY

When avalanches make the news, it's usually a case of one or two skiers, snowboarders, or snowmobilers getting caught in a slide. Less common are avalanches that rumble into—and sometimes through—a town, demolishing buildings and other infrastructure. But that's what happened to several towns on one March night in 1911.

On the dry, east side of the Sierra Nevada, Mill Creek tumbles from the 12,000-foot crest into Lundy Canyon, a narrow valley lined on both sides with ragged, steep-walled mountains. Toward the mouth of this canyon, the northern wall rises to a ridge topped by Mount Olsen and Copper Mountain. The latter takes its name from the copper ore that miners pursued in the area after gold mines petered out. In the late 1800s, mining camps grew into small towns at the base of Copper Mountain—Lundy, Jordan, and Mono City, just north and west of Mono Lake.

The town of Lundy was organized in 1879 following several gold strikes in the area. It was a thriving community with saloons, boarding-houses, and hotels. There was a ten-stamp mill for grinding the ore from the mines. The May Lundy Mine, located in the Homer Mining District, was the chief source of gold in the area. It was one of the few mines that paid off handsomely.

The mining town of Lundy, circa 1890, nestled below
the steep slopes of the eastern Sierra Nevada.
PHOTOGRAPH IN PUBLIC DOMAIN.

Eventually, the costs of mining outweighed the profits, so by 1884 the May Lundy Mine suspended operations and the town of Lundy went into decline. In 1900, the Crystal Lake Mining Company purchased the mine. Power was supplied by a hydroelectric plant with a Pelton wheel on Mill Creek, two miles south of the mill. A power line ran between the power plant and the mill. Although the mine reopened at intervals for a few more years, its heyday was over.

Strong winds and heavy snowfalls came to Mono County throughout the winter of 1911. Temperatures often fell to twenty degrees below zero. Roads from one settlement to another were closed for days. Life was never easy in these mining and lumbering towns, but that year was especially hard. The secretary for the power company lived in Bodie, twenty miles northeast of Lundy. One night, she decided to walk downtown to the Occidental Hotel for dinner. The snow was so deep that she had to duck to pass beneath the power lines on their tall poles. Snow falling off roofs made huge piles on the sidewalks, which were also icy. At one point, she slipped, slid down the slope and across the street, and went right through the window into the dining room of the hotel, taking the window frame with her.

On March 6, another heavy snow began. It continued snowing hard the next day, and four men who lived in Bodie near the lumber office decided to walk a quarter of a mile to the hotel to wait out the storm. It took them four hours to reach Main Street, where they found the snow in places to be as high as the rooftops. The town of Bodie was dark—residents deduced that a power line had broken in the storm.

The mines in Bodie had been running on electricity since 1893, but electrical power was not available for large portions of the town. So there had been a great deal of excitement in April 1910 when construction began on a hydroelectric plant in Jordan, near the eastern foot of Copper Mountain. Plans called for the new power plant to be in operation by August. It would supply electricity to many small towns in California and Nevada. But the project dragged on, and it wasn't until Christmas 1910 that the whole town of Bodie finally had electricity from the new power plant. Now, suddenly, the town was dark again. Not knowing what had happened, people pulled out their old oil lamps.

With roads closed and telephone lines down due to the great accumulations of snow, Bodie had no connection with the outside world for seventeen hours. The townspeople started to dig out the next day when the storm abated. A caretaker at Mono Mills finally made a phone connection and spread the word that avalanches had not only taken out the Jordan power plant, killing employees there, but had also destroyed parts of the town of Lundy and the mining power plant there. The massive slides had also swept away buildings, killing several residents.

Soon news spread of the terror-filled early hours of March 7. Residents of Lundy reported that a tremendous roar had filled the air as an avalanche of snow and rock rushed down the slopes of Copper Mountain and then on down the canyon. It was late at night, and people had been fast asleep. Among them was Jasper Parrot, a hermit who had lived a quiet and isolated life in his shack for thirty years. Another was Robert Mason, chief engineer of the power plant in nearby Jordan. They had no warning of

Men with shovels clear a roof after a heavy snowfall in Lundy.
PHOTOGRAPH IN PUBLIC DOMAIN.

the destruction headed their way. Parrot was swept away in an instant; his body was never found. Mason, too, would not survive the night.

In fact, a series of slides devastated the area that night. They went on for hours, hitting the towns of Jordan, Lundy, and Mono City. The noise of the huge snowslides woke people only when it was too late to flee; survivors said the roaring avalanches could be heard for miles.

The hydroelectric plant at Jordan had been turned over to the Pacific Power Company in January. A pipeline from Lundy, seven miles away, carried some of the water of Mill Creek along the north side of the canyon and around to the east side of Copper Mountain, where there was a fall of 1,500 feet to the powerhouse. The one-story building was made of concrete. There were also concrete cottages to house power-plant employees. These buildings were considered safe since they were located about 1,000 feet from the steep side of the mountain. A smelter in a building nearby had stood since 1879. But that night, the Jordan power-plant building and cottages and the old smelter house were destroyed. Surprisingly, the new machinery inside the power plant was not badly damaged.

How had such widespread destruction happened all at once? So much snow had fallen that the slopes were heavily loaded. Winds formed the snow into deep drifts. One of these had then broken loose, simply too heavy to support itself. Snow started sliding down the mountain, gaining speed and picking up rocks and debris as it swept down. A series of three avalanches struck near the entrance to Lundy Canyon, including one that came down Lundy Canyon itself. The first slide, which occurred at 10 P.M., went through the upper end of the town of Lundy. The second and third slides hit the center and lower end of town. The avalanches carried away the county jail, a butcher shop, and a slaughterhouse, accounting for the deaths of at least four men.

Another flanking group of slides hit the hydroelectric plant at Jordan, killing four engineers, including chief engineer Mason, and carrying away his wife, Agnes. The destruction of the Jordan power plant left the towns of Bodie, Lucky Boy, and Hawthorne without power and cast gloom over future plans to furnish power to the mines and mills in the area, even as far away as Wonder, Nevada, forty miles east of Fallon. The slides swept people, their homes, and all kinds of equipment and supplies down the mountain to the very edge of Mono Lake. The post office at Mono City was destroyed.

When news of the avalanches got out, rescuers from Bodie and Lee Vining mobilized to search for victims. Established in 1852 as a mining camp, Lee Vining sits on the southwestern shore of Mono Lake. Roads were impassable, so the rescuers were forced to come by skis or snowshoes. One rescue group found Agnes Mason still alive sixty-four hours after she'd been swept away in her bed during the night. She was in critical condition. Her dog, still with her, was fine. Eight skiers pulling a toboggan took Agnes twenty miles to Bodie. Although her injuries were severe, she did survive. Searchers worked for several days after the avalanches to find and identify the victims.

Today, near the site of the avalanches, the Jordan-Lundy Avalanche Memorial Cemetery holds several of the victims. Each grave has an engraved marker made from stones that were recovered from the destroyed Jordan power plant. There's also a plaque on U.S. Highway 395 at Mill Creek Powerhouse Road marking the site of the disaster. This plaque was dedicated on September 10, 2011, by the Bodie Chapter No. 64 of E Clampus Vitus, a fraternal organization dedicated to preserving western mining history.

ALPINE MEADOWS AVALANCHE, 1982

When an avalanche strikes, the clock begins ticking against anyone buried in the snow. About 90 percent of people rescued within the first fifteen minutes survive, but the survival rate over the next half hour plummets. After forty-five minutes, fewer than 30 percent of victims are found alive. So rescuers were amazed when they uncovered twenty-two-year-old Anna Conrad alive a full five days after a massive avalanche struck Alpine Meadows ski resort near Lake Tahoe on March 31, 1982. Conrad's survival was a rare piece of good news to come out of one of North America's deadliest ski-resort avalanches.

March 1982 certainly went out like a lion. On March 27, a late-season blizzard hit the high Sierras around Lake Tahoe, dumping a foot or more of snow each day for four days straight. By March 31, nearly eight feet of new snow had accumulated on the eighty-seven-inch base at Alpine Meadows. During the storm, ski patrollers carried small explosives on the ski runs and used them to release small slides. They also used a 75-millimeter recoilless cannon and a howitzer on several spots, including The Buttress, a large rock outcrop west of the main lodge and parking lot. The wind and snow were so bad that patrollers could barely see their targets, but they knew from experience where to aim. They fired shell after shell, releasing small slides to reduce the overall hazard.

By noon on March 30, there was so much snow and wind that the ski hill closed to the public. Only a few guests remained in the condos not far downhill from the main lodge. Most of the staff were off duty. The next day, the resort remained closed and the storm strengthened, with winds exceeding 100 miles per hour. The well-respected mountain manager, fifty-two-year-old Bernie Kingery, sent most of the exhausted ski patrollers and other resort employees home. Kingery himself, an avalanche-control veteran with twenty-three years of experience, sat in the avalanche-forecasting office on the bottom floor of the three-story terminal building for the Summit chairlift, near the main lodge. The normally bustling building was also home to the ski school and ski-patrol offices, as well as the resort's main cache of avalanche rescue equipment. That day it was empty except for a handful of employees.

An assistant patrol director, Larry Heywood, and several other ski patrollers traveled to neighboring Squaw Valley ski resort to ride the KT-22 chairlift, so they could ski off the backside toward Alpine Meadows and bomb a few slide paths that threatened the Alpine Meadows Road. Jake Smith, an operations assistant, hopped onto a snowmobile and went to warn motorists not to use the road until the patrollers had released any slides above.

Although this blizzard was fierce, Alpine Meadows was accustomed to big storms and heavy snowfalls. The resort had opened in December 1961. It quickly gained fame for its 2,000 acres of slopes, glades, and bowls. Its runs ranged from tame to expert and offered views of beautiful Lake Tahoe to the east. With a base elevation of 6,835 feet and a summit at 8,637 feet, Alpine Meadows almost always boasted a good snowpack. But the wealth of snow also poses a hazard: on average, Alpine Meadows experiences more avalanches each year than any other ski resort in the United States.

By midafternoon, the resort was almost empty except for a handful of employees. But a few guests were antsy with cabin fever after being cooped up in their condos for four days. Dr. Leroy Nelson, an orthopedic surgeon from Eureka, California, decided to walk to the lodge to look for food. A neighbor, David Hahn, tagged along. Hahn, Nelson, his wife Katie, and their eleven-year-old daughter Laura slowly made their way through deep snow toward the lodge. They paused at one point to watch a snowplow at work. Katie then turned around and went back to the condo, where the couple's son, Eric, was waiting. Hahn, Dr. Nelson, and his daughter continued toward the lodge. When they reached the parking area by the lodge, they met Jake Smith on his snowmobile.

Just then, at 3:45 P.M., a large, soft-slab avalanche released from the Buttress, Pond, and Poma Rocks slide paths. Smith saw it coming and made a desperate radio call to Kingery. A single word came through on Kingery's end—"Avalanche!" The massive slide swept 800 feet down-hill, snapping off full-grown trees as it went and totally destroying the three-story Summit chairlift terminal building. Mixed with debris from the terminal building, the slide slammed into the lodge, collapsing a wall. A twenty-foot wall of snow roared across the parking area and down the road, catching Smith, Hahn, Dr. Nelson, and his daughter. The avalanche also damaged two other chairlifts, several snowcats, and a few outbuildings before coming to a halt.

Besides Kingery, a handful of people were in the Summit chairlift terminal building when the slide hit. Twenty-two-year-old Beth Morrow assisted Kingery with monitoring radio communications. The others were Randy Buck, Tad DeFelice, and Jeff Skover, all employees at Alpine Meadows. Anna Conrad and her boyfriend, Frank Yeatman, were gathering clothes in a locker room on the second floor. (Yeatman had driven up from the University of California-Davis, unaware of how bad the storm had become.)

As the avalanche settled, the lights at the ski resort flickered and went out. When the avalanche hit the main ski lodge, it broke all the windows. Snow filled the lounge, the cafeteria, and all of the second floor. The fire sprinkler system came on, soaking everything with icy cold water. Remarkably, all the people in the lodge survived.

When Larry Heywood and his team of ski patrollers reached the top of the KT-22 chairlift at Squaw Valley, someone ran up to them with the worrisome news that an avalanche had just destroyed homes in the neighborhood near the base of Squaw Valley. If slides were happening at Squaw Valley, then Alpine Meadows was ripe for trouble. They radioed the Alpine Meadows headquarters and got no response, so they began skiing down toward Alpine Meadows. When Heywood finally reached the Alpine Meadows parking lot, he was still on his skis but being pulled by a snowcat.

The base of the ski hill was unrecognizable. As other employees and rescuers arrived at the scene, everyone was stunned by the devastation. Heywood observed, "This was no ordinary slide, but a once-in-a-century catastrophe."

Randy Buck, who was in the terminal building when the avalanche hit, said, "You could hear a rumble and then the building started to shake. Violently. Then there was an air blast." Buck hit the floor, curled up into a ball, and was instantly covered in snow as he was carried across the room. When the slide stopped, Buck found himself buried under a foot and a half of hardpacked snow. He dug himself out despite having suffered broken ribs and vertebrae. As he looked around, still dazed, he saw that the walls of the room he had been in moments before were gone. He found another employee who had survived but was buried nearby in the snow. Buck was able to partially uncover the victim but not completely free him.

Word spread quickly, and more help began to arrive. The road into the ski resort was impassable due to downed tree limbs and debris. Power lines and telephone poles were down. Rescuers rode in on snowcats. They soon freed the man still caught in the snow in the Summit terminal building. In the growing darkness, rescuers used headlamps to continue the search for victims. They needed probes to search through the deep snow in the parking lot, but probes and other equipment had been stored in the terminal building, which had been destroyed. Improvised probes were made from electrical conduit that had been pre-cut into twenty-foot lengths and stored in the still-intact maintenance building.

The next morning, the weather had greatly improved. More than ninety people joined in the search for those still missing. They found another body: Anna Conrad's boyfriend, Frank Yeatman. There had been no sign of either of them since the avalanche hit. As the rescuers frantically searched, they picked up a signal from an avalanche beacon. Following the signal, they found another body, that of an employee who had been wearing her transmitter when smothered

On Friday, more snow fell in the Sierras. In spite of the snow and wind, and with fading hopes that either of the last two people still missing would be found alive, the rescue teams continued to work. Also missing was a search dog that belonged to an avalanche forecaster at the resort. The dog was found a bit banged up but alive. The dog's owner was in the small group that found him and was delighted. Hopes for finding the last two people alive were dashed as the weather turned bad again for the next three days. In that time the area received another forty inches of snow.

The new snow increased the risk of another avalanche above the search site, so rescue efforts were temporarily halted. On Monday, April 5, the weather improved slightly, and searchers again probed the area around the terminal building for the two employees still missing. Among the searchers from the U.S. Forest Service were Don and Roberta Huber and their search dogs, Blackie and Bridget. Shortly after 1 P.M., Roberta's dog, Bridget, became excited. She wagged her tail, barked, and nosed around in the snow. Seconds later, as they dug near that spot, rescuers spied the hand of Anna Conrad. Remarkably, Anna was conscious and talking. Two hours later, rescuers found the body of the last victim, mountain manager Bernie Kingery, next to the tree that held the ski-school bell. The long search was over.

Conrad described how the avalanche had blasted into the locker room, knocking down the wall and lockers. She fell beneath one of the benches, which saved her from being crushed by the toppled wall. In turn, the fallen wall created an air space around her. Conrad didn't realize what had happened. She said she thought she'd been caught in an explosion. "I had absolutely no idea what had happened," she said. "It was so instantaneous. I did a lot of sleeping and thinking about friends. I just kept telling myself I could do it. I could do it. They'd find me." She had a black eye and numerous bruises.

When the slide hit, Conrad had been wearing a sweater and ski pants. From the locker above her, she pulled out a down jacket, a hat, and gloves and put them on. She also had on woolen socks and cross-country ski boots. Still, after being trapped for days in her freezing tomb of snow, her feet had become badly frostbitten. She said that, on the third day, she thought she heard rescuers' voices and screamed for help, but no one responded. She had nothing to eat but snow. There was no light, but she kept track of the days by the sound of the blasts each morning as patrollers dynamited avalanche paths.

Conrad was taken by helicopter to Tahoe Forest Hospital in Truckee. The doctors there performed surgery to increase circulation in an attempt to save her legs and feet. She remained under care there for two months and underwent several more surgeries. As a result of her ordeal, she lost her right leg below the knee and the toes and a part of her left foot from frostbite. After recovering from her surgeries, Conrad was fitted with a prosthesis. She began skiing again the following December. She returned to school, earned a teaching certificate, and taught high school science in the Bay Area for a time. Then she moved back to the mountains she loved. She eventually married and had children, settling with her family in Mammoth Lakes, where she worked at the ski resort.

The rescue of Anna Conrad made headlines. There was also considerable excitement about Bridget, the nine-year-old German shepherd that had previously played a role in seventy searches. Bridget was part of a California search-and-rescue dog group called Wilderness Finders, or WOOF. This group had taken part in a variety of searches but had never found a live victim at an avalanche site. Previously, by the time the group was contacted and the owners and dogs arrived on the scene, valuable time had passed and the avalanche victims that were found were no longer alive. This time Bridget had located a live victim beneath the snow. This was the first time in North America that a live avalanche victim had been found by any search-and-rescue dog.

The Alpine Meadows avalanche took a somber tally. Seven people died and five were severely injured. It's considered one of the biggest disasters in North American ski history. The monetary loss from the avalanche was estimated at $1.6 million in 1982 dollars. Families of the victims sued Alpine Meadows for wrongful death. They questioned whether the warnings and avalanche-control measures had been adequate. Several avalanche consultants were called to testify, and they presented many conflicting perspectives during the five-month trial. The jury deliberated for two and a half weeks before giving its final verdict that the ski resort was not negligent.

The Alpine Meadows avalanche spurred several positive undertakings. The resort built earthen berms to protect the parking lot and lodge from future avalanches. And on a broader scale the disaster led to the creation of the nonprofit Sierra Avalanche Center, affiliated with the U.S. Forest Service. It predicts avalanche danger throughout the greater Lake Tahoe area for backcountry skiers, snowmobilers, and snowboarders.

MONTECITO MUDSLIDES, 2018

Berkeley "Augie" Johnson and his family knew that heavy rains were forecast for their community of Montecito on January 8, 2018. They knew that their home was in a voluntary evacuation zone due to a threat of flooding. But the Johnsons, like many people in the area, had "evacuation fatigue." Throughout December 2017, officials had warned them to be ready to evacuate due to the nearby Thomas Fire—at that time the largest wildfire in California history. Santa Ana winds drove the fire from Ventura north and west, threatening Montecito and nearby Santa Barbara. By January, the fire was contained, and rain seemed like a blessing—it would help extinguish any remaining hot spots. But now officials warned the Johnsons and their neighbors that heavy rains soaking the burned slopes above them could cause flooding and mudslides. Although officials went door to door to alert residents, many of them ignored the warnings.

The Johnsons lived about two miles below Cold Creek. Thinking that it might flood, Augie Johnson decided to put sandbags around the doors of his home before he sat down to dinner. Later, he watched a football game on television and then went to bed. Because the family feared that water might seep into the ground floor, everyone slept upstairs. Johnson awoke to a heavy downpour at about 3:30 A.M. on January 9 and went outside to check the gutters on his roof. He heard a low rumbling sound and looked up the hill. He saw trees breaking and falling. He also saw a swath of mud and boulders sliding toward him.

Johnson raced back inside the house just as the back wall imploded and mud rushed in. He was covered up to his waist, but he made his way upstairs to where his wife, son, and daughter were sleeping. As the house groaned from the force of the flow, wood beams cracked, windows exploded, and boulders ripped away the master bedroom on the main floor. Johnson feared that the second floor might also give way, so he and his family climbed onto the roof. They stood by their chimney and watched boulders tear away chunks of their house. In an interview days after the mudslide, Johnson reported that his son later quipped, "Good thing we put up those sandbags, Dad."

The Johnsons weren't the only ones to lose their home that morning. Mudslides and flash floods devastated Santa Barbara County, scouring stream drainages, spilling into neighborhoods, and destroying everything in their path. Experts had warned of this hazard; they'd explained that California was in a new "fire-flood era" in which wildfires left little but ashen soils in their wake. Seasonal rains could then bring the destabilized mountainsides down in torrents of mud and debris.

This was precisely the scenario that played out in Montecito. In December 2017, the Thomas Fire had burned nearly 440 square miles, scorching slopes and ravines across the Santa Ynez Mountains above Montecito. Without plants and roots to hold the soil in place, the steep hillsides were vulnerable, just waiting for rain and gravity to do their dirty work.

On January 5, 2018, a low-pressure system and cold front developed off the California coast. It moved onto the mainland on January 8, bringing heavy rain to Southern California. The fear of mudslides prompted mandatory evacuations of parts of Los Angeles, Santa Barbara, and Ventura Counties, but low-lying areas weren't included in the mandatory evacuation zone. Few people understood how precarious the circumstances were, and the extent of the deluge was unexpected. Some residents did place sandbags across their driveways or plywood at their front doors. Then the storm intensified over Montecito.

Wildfires denuded steep slopes above Montecito, leaving soil exposed and vulnerable to erosion. PHOTOGRAPH BY JASON KEAN, U.S. GEOLOGICAL SURVEY.

This semi-rural coastal town along U.S. Highway 101 at the foot of the Santa Ynez Mountains was home to just under 9,000 people. Less than 100 miles from Los Angeles and boasting splendid views of the Pacific Ocean, Montecito had attracted wealthy homebuyers, including such Hollywood stars as Oprah Winfrey, Natalie Portman, and Ellen DeGeneres. Land-use planners questioned the wisdom of building neighborhoods on and below such steep mountainsides, but those concerns did little to slow lucrative development.

As heavy rains pounded the Santa Ynez range on January 8 and 9, Montecito received the brunt of it. After hours of steady rain, an estimated half inch fell in just five minutes at 3:30 A.M. on the 9th, triggering torrential mudslides down Cold Spring and San Ysidro Creeks. Rivers of mud, boulders, and trees, in places forming a wall fifteen feet tall, roared into town at twenty miles per hour. Many people awoke to the roar and rumbling thinking it was an earthquake. Some peered out of their bedroom windows and saw an eerie orange glow in the sky. They couldn't believe that the Thomas Fire had come to life again given all the rain, but they also couldn't know the real cause: the mudslides had ruptured a natural-gas line that had then burst into flames.

Mudflows roared down streambeds, including San Ysidro Creek,
into Montecito, leaving debris and destruction in their path.
PHOTOGRAPH BY JASON KEAN, U.S. GEOLOGICAL SURVEY.

Montecito resident Ben Hyatt said the mud "came in an instant, like a dam breaking." He rushed to wake his family as the mud slammed into their home, banging into doors and walls. Throughout town, the noise drew many people outside to see what was causing all the commotion. Hannah Troy stepped outside only to realize that her Toyota minivan, which had been parked on the street, was gone, replaced by mud and debris. She went back inside and waited for rescuers to arrive. Sixty-nine-year-old Josie Gower was less fortunate; she opened her front door only to be swept away by mud. Her body was recovered the next day.

Over the next few days, the extent of the disaster became clear. The mudslides had destroyed sixty-five homes and damaged hundreds more. Mud two to fifteen feet deep filled homes, yards, and roads. More than 20,000 people were without electricity. A thirty-mile section of U.S. Highway 101 between Santa Barbara and Ventura was closed until crews could clear debris.

Help began to pour into Montecito. More than 1,250 firefighters from California and other states as well as members of the California National Guard came to assist in search and rescue missions. Rescuers rode in the shovels of large excavators to reach survivors. When a helicopter crew spotted one fourteen-year-old girl trapped in the mud, it took firefighters two hours to reach her and pull her to safety.

Gradually, the rescue efforts switched to body recovery searches. And then people began an enormous cleanup effort. A big job was dealing with the many massive boulders smashed against homes or blocking roads. The rocks, up to twelve feet in diameter, were too big to move in one piece, so experienced blasters from the California Department of Transportation were brought in. Over a two-day period, crews drilled bore holes and planted explosives to blast twelve of these monster boulders. Because the boulders were composed of sandstone, the explosions fractured the huge rocks but didn't send fragments flying through the air. In other places, near gas lines where an explosion would be too dangerous, an expanding gel was injected into the boulders, causing them to crack open after a few hours.

All told, the mudslides killed 23 people and seriously injured 173 more. Two people were never found. The dead ranged in age from three to eighty-nine years old. Property damage was estimated to be at least $177 million, with an additional $7 million in emergency-response costs and $43 million in cleanup costs.

With its mountains bare of trees and vegetation for years to come, Montecito remains at risk from future mudslides. As wildfires continue to ravage California and seasonal rains return each year, the Montecito mudslides of 2018 have many property owners looking warily to the hills above their homes, wondering what their own futures will be.

Boulders of all sizes and a thick layer of mud filled yards.
PHOTOGRAPH BY JASON KEAN, U.S. GEOLOGICAL SURVEY.

SOURCES

Snow and Rock Avalanches Strike Mono County

E Clampus Vitus, Bodie Chapter No. 64. Avalanche of 1911 (roadside historic plaque). Dedicated September 10, 2011.

Lundy, California. Western Mining History. https://westernmininghistory.com/towns/california/lundy/

Nevada State Journal. "People Perish in Terrible Avalanche Snow." March 8, 1911.

U.S. Geological Survey. May Lundy Mine. Mineral Resource Data System.

Vargo, Cecile Page. "Christmas Delivery at Bodie Sparks Jordan Disaster." *Explore Historic California.* December 2001.

Alpine Meadows Avalanche

Bunker, David. "25 years ago: Alpine avalanche of '82 not forgotten around basin." *Tahoe Daily Tribune.* April 1, 2007.

Ellison, Patti. "Avalanche Survivor Buried Nearly 5 Days." *North Lake Tahoe Bonanza.* April 7, 1982.

McLaughlin, Mark. "Tahoe Nuggets: 30 Years Ago, Alpine Meadows Avalanche." Tahoetopia.com.

Weiss, Claire. "35 Years Since Deadly Alpine Meadows, CA Avalanche." *Snow Brains.* March 31, 2017.

Woodlief, Jennifer. *A Wall of White: The True Story of Heroism and Survival in the Face of a Deadly Avalanche.* New York, NY: Atria Books, a Division of Simon & Schuster, Inc., 2009.

Montecito Mudslides

Biasotti, Tony, Max Ufberg, and Scott Wilson. " 'Evacuation fatigue' caused some to ignore peril of mudslides." *The Washington Post.* January 11, 2018.

Bizjak, Tony. "In new California era of 'fire-floods,' where will deadly debris flows strike next?" *Ventura County Star.* November 3, 2018.

Boyle, T. Coraghessan. "After the Mudslides, an Absence in Montecito." *The New Yorker.* January 22, 2018.

Cullen, Andrew. "Mudslides Strike California." *The New York Times*. January 16, 2018.

Dobuzinskis, Alex. " 'Window closing' for California mudslide searchers as death toll rises to 18." Reuters. January 12, 2018.

Edhat staff. "Montecito man details mudslide experience on the Ellen show." January 24, 2018.

Karimi, Faith, Steve Almasy, and Dakin Andone. "California mudslides: Death toll rises to 20, 4 still missing." CNN. January 15, 2018.

Knoll, Corina. "After the Montecito mudslides, a search for belongings and two children." *Los Angeles Times*. October 1, 2018.

Lee, Jasmine C., Jennifer Medina, and Alicia Parlapiano. "Identifying the Causes of the California Mudslides." *The New York Times*. January 16, 2018.

Mozingo, Joe. "Santa Barbara County knew mudslides were a risk. Did little to stop them." *Los Angeles Times*. December 20, 2018.

Mozingo, Joe, Brittny Mejia, and Matt Hamilton. "Mud, darkness and destruction turned Montecito into death trap." *Los Angeles Times*. January 16, 2018.

Serna, Joseph. "How a group of scientists are using the deadly Montecito mudflow to predict future disasters." *Los Angeles Times*. February 7, 2018.

Serna, Joseph and Javier Panzar. "Crew uses explosives to blast boulders plugging creeks in Montecito." *Los Angeles Times*. January 17, 2018.

LASSEN PEAK ERUPTS

IN MID-JUNE 1914, THREE MEN CLIMBED TO THE TOP OF LASSEN PEAK in California's northeast corner. They were curious because, for the previous sixteen days, the dormant volcano had rumbled and spit gas and ash. No one alive had ever seen or heard any discernible activity from Lassen. Now, as the men looked down into a newborn crater, they felt the earth tremble. The men quickly turned and began to run back down the mountain. Rocks and ash spewed into the air. A rock struck one of the men and knocked him down. Perhaps they'd chosen the wrong moment to climb Lassen Peak—and perhaps they would pay with their lives. Then, as suddenly as it had started, the eruption stopped. These three lucky men survived.

Three men explore a newly formed crater on Lassen Peak in June 1914.
PHOTOGRAPH BY J. L. BRAMBILLA, COURTESY OF THE U.S. GEOLOGICAL SURVEY.

Earlier that spring, on May 30, Lassen Peak had experienced an abrupt steam explosion that created a small crater at the summit. The crater grew as 170 additional small explosions occurred over the next eleven months, until the crater measured 1,000 feet across. Steam explosions are caused when water (in this case from snowmelt and rain) contacts molten rock and instantly turns into super-heated steam. In a split second, the water molecules expand by as much as 1,700 times their original volume, producing powerful explosions. If steam explosions were occurring on Lassen, it could only mean that lava was building up beneath the peak.

A year later, on May 14, 1915, people noticed that the top of Lassen Peak was glowing. The glow could be seen from towns twenty miles away. Lava had emerged within the summit crater. Soon, a lava dome filled the crater, and on May 19 it exploded. Chunks of the lava dome were ejected and lava spilled over the edge of the crater. Its heat generated small mudflows down the sides of Lassen Peak. Some lava spilled 1,000 feet down the northwest rim, causing a modest mudflow. Late that night, molten

A steam explosion on Lassen Peak in 1914.
PHOTOGRAPH BY BENJAMIN F. LOOMIS, COURTESY OF THE U.S. GEOLOGICAL SURVEY.

lava and hot rocks flowed onto the northeast slope and hit layers of ash and snow thirty feet deep. The ash had been deposited by previous minor explosions, and the snow had accumulated during a severe winter. A gigantic mudflow made up of water, snow, ash, lava, and rock started down the slopes of the mountain.

This initial mudflow was somewhat cooler than a pyroclastic flow (a mix of hot gases and rocks) and a little drier than a lahar (a slurry of rocks, debris, and water). It ripped up everything in its path. As it flowed, it picked up additional debris and water from melted snow and became a lahar. At its beginning, the mudflow was about twenty feet deep, and at the end it left a deposit about six feet deep. Both the avalanche and the lahar released a flood of muddy water into Lost Creek and the Hat Creek Valley.

Elmer Sorahan, one of the ranchers living there, was awakened around midnight by his frantically barking dog. Sorahan dressed and went out expecting to find some kind of wild animal harassing his livestock. Instead,

Eruptive activity melted snow and ice high on Lassen Peak,
unleashing mudflows like this one.
PHOTOGRAPH BY P. J. THOMPSON, COURTESY OF THE U.S. GEOLOGICAL SURVEY.

according to a U.S. Geological Survey report, he saw a twelve-foot-high wall of logs and muddy water slowly creeping down the creek. This mixture was much thicker than water; it was more like mortar, flowing about seven miles per hour. As fast as he could, he ran more than a mile to his neighbors' house to alert them that a flood was coming. His neighbors, the Halls, quickly phoned a warning to others and then rushed outside just before their home was swept away. Other houses downstream were also destroyed. Thanks to Sorahan's dog and the rancher's quick action, no lives were lost. The floodwaters continued another thirty miles to Pit Creek. There, the muddy waters killed many of the fish in the streams.

By the morning of May 20, lava began to collect again in the crater on top of Lassen Peak. The crater filled slowly and pressure built over the next two days. Then, at about 4 P.M. on May 22, a huge explosion threw rocks and pumice high into the air. This was Lassen's largest eruption during the swarm that took place between 1914 and 1917. It rained ash for miles. Over the next half hour, a huge column of volcanic ash and gas rose in the air to a height of 30,000 feet. The column was visible 150 miles to the west in Eureka, California, and it rained fine ash on Winnemucca, Nevada, 200 miles to the east.

The May 22, 1915, eruption sent a towering column of ash and gas into the atmosphere.
PHOTOGRAPH BY R. E. STINSON, COURTESY OF THE U.S. GEOLOGICAL SURVEY.

When some of the column fell back onto the northeast slope of Lassen Peak, it created what is called a pyroclastic flow, made up of hot ash, pumice, rocks, and gases. It flowed at great speed along the ground, knocking down any remaining standing trees, scorching timber, and starting at least one small wildfire. As the flow picked up water from the snow that melted beneath it, it became a lahar that flowed fifteen miles down Lost Creek. Once again, the flow landed in lower Hat Creek. Smaller mudflows ran down all flanks of Lassen Peak.

Then Lassen Peak grew quiet, although a few steam explosions continued over the next couple of years. Although these eruptions were unexpected, the region has a long history of volcanic action. Scientists suggest that—600,000 to 400,000 years ago—eruptions built up Mount Tehama, or Brokeoff Volcano, which was about the same size as Mount St. Helens in Washington. Over the years, Tehama became inactive and eroded away through glacial activity, leaving remnants that include today's Brokeoff Mountain, Mount Conard, Mount Diller, and Diamond Peak. Eruptions from this volcanic center formed Lassen Peak about 27,000 years ago.

Lassen Peak still shows scars from its eruptions of 1915 to 1917. The eruptions blasted a three-mile area on the northeast side of Lassen Peak, today known as the "Devastated Area" within Lassen Volcanic National Park. A nature trail affords visitors a close-up view of the once-barren area that is now filling in with plants and trees. The first trees to come back were aspens. In the region are several huge rocks that were ejected from the volcano. The best known of these is called "Hot Rock," conveniently located near California Highway 89 east of the Chaos Crags. The avalanche on May 19 created and then carried this 300-ton rock four and a half miles down the mountain. This lava rock when molten could have reached 1,650 degrees Fahrenheit. It was still hot for days after it came to rest.

The hydrothermal features of Lassen Volcanic National Park are reminders that there's still volcanic activity there. These features include fumaroles or vents, mud pots, boiling pools, and hot ground. Molten or nearly molten volcanic rock lies several miles below the surface. Visitors often notice an odor from hydrogen sulfide that is much like the smell of rotten eggs.

The largest and most popular of the hydrothermal sections of Lassen Volcanic Park is Bumpass Hell. It's the best place to see emissions of steam and volcanic gases from the Lassen hydrothermal system. Big Boiler is the largest fumarole there, and the steam jetting from it has been measured at 322 degrees Fahrenheit, making it one of the hottest fumaroles in the world. In spring, when there's cooler underground water from snowmelt, the temperature in the fumaroles and pools is lower, and the mud pots are somewhat cooler and thicker.

While this disaster was frightening, no human lives were lost because the area at that time was so sparsely populated. Fish were killed, and there was some environmental destruction. Now warning systems are in place to alert local residents of an eruption should Lassen reawaken.

Lassen Peak is part of the Cascade Volcanic Arc, which stretches from southwest British Columbia to Northern California. It was named in honor of a Danish blacksmith, Peter Lassen, who served as a guide in the 1800s for immigrants passing the peak on their way to the Sacramento Valley in California. The peak, located in Shasta County about fifty-five miles east of the town of Redding, soars to 10,457 feet. It's surrounded by its namesake national park and also by Lassen National Forest. Its lava dome is one of the largest on earth. Lassen Peak receives more snowfall than anywhere else in California. The average annual snowfall is 600 inches, and in some years it has reached 1,000 inches.

In 1907, President Theodore Roosevelt designated two national monuments: Cinder Cone and Lassen Peak. Because of the volcanic eruptions starting in 1914 and the attention they focused on the region, Lassen Peak and Cinder Cone and the area immediately around them were designated Lassen Volcanic National Park on August 9, 1916. The park was established in part to preserve the area for scientific study of the eruptions' impacts on the landscape. The main road through the new national park was constructed between 1925 and 1931. Parts of the road are 8,512 feet above sea level, and it's not unusual for the road to be covered in twelve feet of snow and to remain closed to regular vehicle traffic until the Fourth of July.

Because of hazards posed by rockslides, earthquakes, and volcanic activity, the visitor center and accommodations that once stood near Manzanita Lake have been closed. A campground, store, and small museum remain. One of those who worked hard for the establishment of this national park was a local businessman named Benjamin Franklin Loomis. He photographed and documented the 1914–1917 eruptions using an 8-by-10-inch camera with glass plate negatives. He made his own film and set up a darkroom in a tent. He published the pictures in a 1926 book, *Pictorial History of the Lassen Volcano*. Some of his work is on display in the museum, which he and his wife financed and dedicated to the memory of their only daughter. In 1929, they donated the Mae Loomis Memorial Museum to the park.

The California Volcanic Observatory in Lassen Volcanic National Park uses a network of sensitive instruments to detect the emission of gases or any significant ground deformations that would warn of future volcanic activity in the region. The geologic history of the area suggests that there are long periods of time between volcanic eruptions, but it's almost certain that this hot spot beneath the Earth's crust will come to life again someday.

SOURCES

Eruptions of Lassen Peak, California, 1914 to 1917. U.S. Geological Survey Fact Sheet 173-98. U.S. Geological Survey.

"Hot Water" in Lassen Volcanic National Park—Fumaroles, Steaming Ground, and Boiling Mudpots. U.S. Geological Survey Fact Sheet 101-02. U.S. Geological Survey.

Klemetti, Erik. "Remembering Lassen Peak's Blast, 100 Years Later." *Wired*. May 20, 2015.

Loomis, B. F. *Pictorial History of the Lassen Volcano*. Mineral, CA: Loomis Museum Association, 1926.

Schaffer, Jeffrey P. *Lassen Volcanic National Park and Vicinity*. Berkeley, CA: Wilderness Press, 1981.

Volcano Hazards of the Lassen Volcanic National Park Area, California. U.S. Geological Survey Fact Sheet 022-00. U.S. Geological Survey.

THE ARGONAUT GOLD MINE FIRE

IN 1850, TWO FREED SLAVES, JAMES HAGER AND WILLIAM TUDOR, discovered gold in the foothills southeast of Sacramento. They worked their mine until the 1860s. The Argonaut Mining Company bought the mine in 1893 and continued pursuing the vein. The Argonaut and the nearby Kennedy Mine were rivals, as well as the main employers for the small town of Jackson, the seat of Amador County. They kept ore-crushing machines working around the clock. By 1920, the main shaft of the Argonaut Mine extended 4,900 feet underground. It was one of the deepest and richest mines in the state. A network of interconnected tunnels and shafts laced through the mine. Two tunnels connected the Argonaut and Kennedy Mines, but they were closed by a fire in 1919.

Many of the mine workers at the Argonaut in the 1920s were immigrants from Italy, Spain, and Serbia. In fact, there were so many Serbs that Jackson had the first Serbian church in the West. These miners earned about $4 a day. Most of the mines in the area ran two or three shifts a day. Under normal operations, the Argonaut Mine ran two shifts: one from 7:30 A.M. to 3:30 P.M. and a night shift from 5:30 P.M. to 1:30 A.M.

The Argonaut Mine and mill, circa 1920, was one of California's deepest and richest mines.
PHOTOGRAPH IN THE PUBLIC DOMAIN.

On August 27, 1922, the hoist engineer lowered the Sunday night shift of men right on time. He distributed the men to three working levels: 4,400, 4,600, and 4,800 feet below the surface. Then at 6 P.M., he lowered the shift boss, Clarence Bradshaw.

At 10:40 P.M., the skip tender was lowered down into the mine to distribute lunch boxes and kegs of water to the miners. After the men had eaten, they went back to work. The shift boss later reported that he first smelled smoke while at the 4,200-foot level at 11:40 P.M. He called to the two men working near him, and they ran for the shaft through increasingly thick smoke. They were raised to the 3,000-foot level, just above the fire.

One of the men got off to remain, observe, and report. The shift boss and the other man were raised to 2,000 feet, where they phoned the hoist engineer to report what was happening. A miner broke in on the call to report that there was smoke at a lower level. This was the last communication with any of the trapped miners. The shift boss and one man were hauled up. Just as they reached the surface, the telephone, bell-signal system, and lights in the mine went out. The shift boss got the foreman and the two of them started back down into the mine. At the 2,800-foot level, they turned back because of smoke and fire.

Word of the disaster quickly spread. The president of the Amador County Chapter of the American Red Cross received word a few hours after the mine fire began. By sunrise, twenty Red Cross workers had taken over a building on the mining property and established a full-service canteen and first-aid station. Their immediate concern was the families of the trapped miners. Family members began arriving at the mine eager for any news. Red Cross workers provided cots, chairs, meals, coffee, and other supplies to the families and rescue workers around the clock. Most importantly, they supplied moral support. Family members were worried and despondent. One threatened to jump down the mine shaft.

Firefighters, townspeople, and miners throughout Amador County arrived on the scene to help. Everyone wanted to do something, large or small. Some offered food and child care. The Bureau of Mines safety station at the University of California-Berkeley was notified and dispatched two trucks equipped with breathing apparatus, rescue equipment, and trained personnel. The city of Elko, Nevada, sent a mine-rescue railroad car with equipment and personnel. Others, including members of the Salvation Army, came to help with food for rescuers and miners' families. One four-year-old girl offered her pet canary to detect poisonous gas in the mine.

Red Cross workers kept cages of canaries near the mine entrance. Atop the cages were grapes for the little birds. As rescuers entered the mine for a shift of backbreaking work in intense heat to clear a path to the trapped men, they carried oxygen tanks. One man in each group also carried a caged canary, which would be more sensitive to deadly carbon monoxide gas created by timbers burning in the mine fire. The death of a canary signaled the rescuers that the tunnel air was unsafe and they should pull on their oxygen masks.

Somewhat disorganized rescue attempts began. Mine officials and government advisors argued over whether to leave the mine ventilating system on or turn it off. A key part of the system was a huge fan at the top of the nearby Muldoon Mine shaft. This fan drew air into the Argonaut Mine by pulling it up the shaft of the old Muldoon mine. But no one knew if this would bring fresh air to the trapped miners or fan the flames. What was the best course of action to help the trapped men?

Mary Warrington, with the Red Cross, talks with employees of the Argonaut Mine during rescue operations in 1922.
PHOTOGRAPH COURTESY OF THE LIBRARY OF CONGRESS, LC-A6197- RC-12179.

It was decided to leave the ventilating system on. When some of the smoke-laden air was drawn out of the main Argonaut shaft and expelled through the Muldoon shaft, firefighters could see the fire below, which had been obscured by smoke. A supply of water was piped to the top of the shaft and delivered through a hose carried by firefighters down to a point where they could direct water onto the fire. Unfortunately, the fire still raged beyond their reach. Out of sight of the firefighters, flames at the lower level continued as evidenced by the black smoke that poured through the Muldoon Mine.

Rescuers with oxygen tanks, called the "Fresh Air Boys," were ready to dig to the trapped men. But there was disagreement over how the rescuers should proceed. Should rescue be attempted through the damaged Argonaut main shaft or through the tunnels that had once connected the Argonaut and Kennedy Mines? On the third day of rescue attempts, it was decided that the best hope of rescue was to reach the lower levels of the Argonaut Mine through tunnels at the lower level of the Kennedy Mine. It was estimated that the rescuers would need to excavate 1,500 feet of the tunnel that had collapsed in the 1919 fire. Mine operators offered a $5,000 reward to the team that first reached the trapped miners.

At first rescuers were limited to two hours of work, and much of this time was taken up simply getting to and from the spot far underground where they had to begin digging. Then rescue workers went to six-hour shifts. They had to use oxygen tanks and work in dim light. Progress was slow. Although Prohibition was in effect, the Red Cross gave rescue workers coming on and off shift a glass of high-quality bourbon, provided by the government. They also handed out cigarettes to those coming off shift.

As anxious relatives and friends of the forty-seven men trapped in the mine waited for news, reporters and cameramen from all over the country began pouring into Jackson. (Among them were eight women reporters, the most women to have covered an event in California since the 1906 earthquake.) On the fifth day of rescue attempts, the Stockton *Record* newspaper ran a story saying that rats by the hundreds were fleeing the Argonaut Mine. Poisonous gases from the lower levels were driving them out. This news greatly reduced hopes that the miners would be found alive.

The rescuers continued their backbreaking work in the Kennedy Mine. Rather than lay tracks and use ore cars to carry out the debris, the men used wheelbarrows to haul the rock they were digging out of the tunnel. The digging went on for weeks. Finally, on the afternoon of Monday, September 18, the rescuers broke through to the Argonaut Mine tunnel. They found a bulkhead that had been built by the trapped miners. The gas was so poisonous at this spot that the rescuers' caged canary dropped dead from its perch. Using gas masks, they continued another twenty-five feet to where they found a second bulkhead. The chinks in this one had been stuffed with pieces of clothing in a vain attempt to keep out the carbon monoxide. The rescue team broke through and found two bodies huddled together. They were father and son Charles and Arthur O'Berg. Nearby, they found the bodies of all the other miners but one. The rescuers could see that the miners had retreated farther into the mine, trying to escape the fire and gas. Their bodies were almost a mile from the mine entrance. A twenty-two-day search had finally ended.

Trapped miner William Fessel scrawled a final message
on the rock before being overcome by toxic gas.
PHOTOGRAPH COURTESY OF THE LIBRARY OF CONGRESS, LC-USZ62-65259.

The trapped miners had nothing with them on which to write messages to their friends and loved ones, but one of the miners, William Fessel, used soot from his carbide lamp to make a brief message on a rock. It read, "3 o/clock., gas getting strong." Now everyone knew that the miners had died very shortly after the fire broke out. The more than 100 reporters in town wrote about the ending of the search, tragic news that was sent on wire services throughout the world.

Red Cross workers took on the task of notifying families of the miners' deaths. Funerals for all the men were held four days later, and although the body of one miner was missing (and would not be found until a year later), forty-seven coffins were buried in the Catholic, Protestant, and Greek Orthodox cemeteries around town. The services were scheduled an hour apart so that grieving friends could attend all of them. In one case, a Catholic miner was buried next to his Protestant friend in the Protestant cemetery. Various dignitaries came and spoke at each of the graveside services.

Speculation swirled as to what had caused this mine fire. Some believed that arson was involved. The mine owners blamed the Wobblies—members of the Industrial Workers of the World union. IWW members had been accused of starting several other mine fires. Others, including some police, wondered if the missing miner, William Fessel, who had left the lone message, might have been the arsonist. The San Francisco chief of police distributed a confidential letter to departments in mining towns throughout the West asking them to contact his office if Fessel was spotted in their community.

Fessel wasn't regarded as a likely suspect by the majority of the mining community in Jackson. He was well liked and respected. He'd lived in the United States for more than twenty years, and there was nothing to make them think that he might be some sort of German spy or arsonist. It was a mystery why his body hadn't been found with the others. A full year later, two miners who were checking a lower level of the Argonaut that had been closed and allowed to fill with water discovered Fessel's body.

A second potential cause of the fire was defective wiring. The fire seemed to have started in the main shaft, where the electric cables ran. There had been reports of some minor electrical problems from the hoist engineer. While the fire could have been caused by a discarded cigarette or a dropped candle, that seemed unlikely because the flames had spread so quickly.

The widows and orphans of the miners killed in the Argonaut Mine received substantial help from various sources. The Amador County Chapter of the American Red Cross collected thousands of dollars in donations from all over the world. Other organizations donated a total of $45,000. The Argonaut Mining Company paid the families back pay and bonuses. The State Compensation Insurance Fund, which insured workers in high-risk industries, also contributed money.

At a coroner's inquest held on September 25, 1922, the shift foreman took the stand and stated that the primary concern immediately after the fire had been detected was to put it out. No one had suggested trying to lower a skip to get the miners out. The hoist operator said he had suggested sending the skip down but the foreman thought it was too late. The hoist operator also said that something was blocking the shaft.

California Governor William D. Stephens appointed a special committee of three to investigate all the facts and conditions surrounding the Argonaut fire. The committee was to determine the cause of the fire and to make appropriate suggestions for future mine safety. Chairman of the committee was A. B. C. Dohrmann, a businessman from San Francisco. Also on the committee were William Loring, a respected mining engineer and major mine operator, and John C. Williams, an experienced gold miner from Grass Valley. This committee first met in San Francisco on September 29. In the weeks that followed, they conducted ten private sessions and four public hearings and spoke with forty-three witnesses.

After listening to all the evidence and hearing conflicting views and observations, the committee concluded that "incendiarism" or defective wiring were the two most likely causes of the fire. They didn't think the fire was accidentally caused by men smoking, by lamp, or by candle. They gave little credence to the rumor that William Fessel, still missing, was an arsonist who caused the disaster.

The committee was highly critical of the shift boss, Clarence Bradshaw, for not informing the men below of their danger and for not shutting off the Muldoon fan, which would have changed the direction of the air flow and directed the fire and smoke upward rather than downward. The committee also thought that Bradshaw shouldn't be severely censored because he hadn't been properly trained on how to proceed when a fire broke out in the mine's main shaft. They recommended thorough training in emergency procedures for all shift bosses and foremen. The committee criticized the mine operators for the lack of fire equipment and training but didn't allege the violation of any mining regulations.

The final report submitted by the committee to the governor contained seventeen recommendations to improve safety in the future. Guided by the information in this report, the state's Industrial Accident Commission amended a section of mine safety orders to become effective the following year. And for the first time, a section titled "Enforcement of Orders" was included, though it didn't include penalties and punishments for violations. In June 1923, the Industrial Accident Commission ordered the Argonaut and Kennedy Mines to construct and maintain a permanent connection between them. Neither mine operator was happy with this ruling, but they didn't contest it, and they did build the required tunnel. Other than this, little of substance changed in mining regulations and safety as a result of the disaster at the Argonaut Mine. It remains the deadliest gold mining disaster in California's history.

SOURCES

DeMarchi, Jane. *Historical Mining Disasters*. Beaver, WV: National Mine Health and Safety Academy, 1997.

Mace, O. Henry. *47 Down, The 1922 Argonaut Gold Mine Disaster*. Hoboken, NJ: John Wiley & Sons, 2004.

Mitchell, Jack. "A Look Back: 95th Anniversary of Argonaut Mining Disaster." *Ledger Dispatch*. August 31, 2017.

Pickard, Byron O. *Lessons from the Fire in the Argonaut Mine*. Washington, D.C.: U.S. Department of Commerce, Bureau of Mines, 1925.

Rasmussen, Cecilia. "1922 Gold Mine Disaster was State's Deadliest." *Los Angeles Times*. January 15, 2006.

THE ST. FRANCIS DAM FAILURE

IN 1877, THE POPULATION OF LOS ANGELES WAS FEWER THAN 10,000 people. By 1930, the city had ballooned to more than 1.2 million. The decades in between span the career of William Mulholland, a self-taught geologist and engineer who envisioned much of the early, extensive infrastructure needed to bring water to this burgeoning City of Angels. Unfortunately, not all went as planned.

Mulholland was born in Belfast, Ireland, in 1855. His working-class parents soon moved back to their hometown of Dublin, where young William attended the O'Connell School. At fifteen, after a beating by his father for poor grades, Mulholland left home and joined the British Merchant Navy. During the next four years as a seaman, he crossed the Atlantic many times to Caribbean and North American ports. In 1874, he landed in New York City and made his way to Michigan, where he worked aboard a Great Lakes freighter and wintered at a lumber camp.

In 1876, Mulholland and his brother, Hugh, sailed as stowaways on a ship from New York bound for California. They were discovered and kicked off the ship in Panama. They walked nearly fifty miles across the isthmus to Balboa on the Pacific and managed to sail once again for

California. They arrived in Los Angeles in 1877. Work was scarce, but Mulholland took a job digging a well. He then prospected for gold in Arizona but returned to Los Angeles and was hired as a ditch tender for the newly formed Los Angeles City Water Company by Frederick Eaton, the company's head officer.

Eaton, about a year younger than Mulholland, harbored political aspirations and dreams of engineering great public works; the two linked their ambitions. Mulholland worked his ditches during the day and taught himself mathematics, geology, hydrology, and engineering at night. Eaton also read up on engineering, and the two men applied what they learned to their jobs at the water company. Mulholland rose through the ranks to become superintendent of the water company by 1886. In 1898, Eaton won election as the mayor of Los Angeles, running on the promise of building a new water supply system for the city. The water company was replaced by the city's own water management agency. By 1902, Mulholland was appointed as the agency's chief engineer and manager.

If Mulholland's trajectory seems like an unlikely rise from school dropout to chief water engineer, bear in mind that this was an era of "self-made" success stories. And it didn't hurt to have allies in positions of power.

In the early years, the city's water supply came from the Los Angeles River and was diverted to the city through a series of ditches. But this basic water system struggled to keep up with explosive growth—from 1880 to 1890, Los Angeles's population more than quadrupled to 50,395, then it doubled again in the next ten years, and then it tripled to nearly 320,000 by 1910. In the face of such growth, Eaton and Mulholland hatched a scheme to divert water from the Owens Valley, east of the Sierra Nevada and 230 miles north of Los Angeles. Eaton bought up land and obtained water rights throughout the Owens Valley, and Mulholland mapped an aqueduct route with a series of reservoirs, canals, covered concrete conduit, and tunnels. Construction began in October 1908 and was completed in November 1913. Gravity alone moved water the entire length of the aqueduct, and the project used the water to generate electricity, making the whole affair cost-effective.

Ranchers and farmers in the Owens Valley were stung by the diversion of local water to a city so far away. They'd been working with the federal Reclamation Service to develop a large irrigation system, and many assumed that Eaton was buying up land and water rights for that project, not to pipe water off to Los Angeles. Eaton didn't discourage their misplaced trust. As Owens Lake dwindled to a dry and dusty alkali pan, the farmers and ranchers took their case to court but lost. Then they rebelled and dynamited portions of the aqueduct to try to prevent what they saw as water theft. Of course, the city simply repaired the damaged aqueduct and continued to siphon "its" water.

But Mulholland was worried by this disruption to the water supply. There were concerns, too, about the susceptibility of the aqueduct to earthquake damage, along with the fact that Owens Lake was drying up faster than originally expected. So Mulholland decided to build a series of five reservoirs to store water for Los Angeles: Haiwee, just south of Owens Lake, and Stone Canyon, Encino, Silver Lake, and Mulholland Dam in the hills immediately north and west of the city. All of these reservoirs continue to supply water to Los Angeles to this day.

Buoyed by these successes, Mulholland moved on to a more ambitious project. He wanted to find a place to safely store a year's supply of water somewhere in Los Angeles County. Mulholland decided to build a dam on San Francisquito Creek, a tributary of the Santa Clara River. This river ran through Los Angeles County to Ventura County, bringing water to communities and farms as it made its way to the Pacific Ocean. Mulholland filed all the paperwork for his proposed dam in Los Angeles County, so people in Ventura County were unaware of the plans being made for "their" river.

By the time people in Santa Paula knew of the plans for the dam, work had already started. The dam was a 205-foot-tall, concrete, arched gravity dam designed and built under Mulholland's direct supervision. At that time, municipally built dams in California weren't regulated and didn't require state inspection. The dam cost $1.3 million to build, coming in under budget. At that time, it was the largest arch-supported dam in the world, built to hold 12 billion gallons (or about 38,000 acre-feet) of water, enough to provide a two-year supply of water for the city of Los Angeles. Once built, Mulholland himself opened the headgate and water began filling the reservoir at the rate of 70 million gallons a day.

Although this project didn't deprive the people in Santa Paula of any water from the Santa Clara River, locals weren't happy. From the beginning, they noticed that the dam leaked. A common comment when planning to next meet a friend was to say, "See you then if the dam don't break."

The dam was built between two rock outcroppings and, even before the dam was finished, water diverted from the aqueduct began to fill the reservoir. Two powerhouses had been built before the dam was constructed to supply electricity to Los Angeles. Powerhouse #1 was built in 1917

William Mulholland designed and built the St. Francis Dam
on San Francisquito Creek to supply water to burgeoning Los Angeles.
PHOTOGRAPH BY HAROLD T. STEARNS, COURTESY OF THE U.S. GEOLOGICAL SURVEY.

and was above the dam site. Six miles away, below the dam site, the second hydroelectric plant, Powerhouse #2, was built in 1920.

A few days before the dam failed, the dam keeper, Tony Harnischfeger, noted some leakage at the base of the dam. He reported this to Mulholland, who came with his chief assistant, Harvey Van Norman, to spend several hours checking the dam. Mulholland apparently was satisfied that there was no urgent threat. He didn't notify others of a danger or send out any alarms. The first inkling local residents had of the impending disaster came just minutes before midnight on March 12, 1928. They felt the earth tremble and heard a rumbling sound. Most assumed that they were experiencing a small earthquake, a fairly common occurrence in the area.

But this was no earthquake. A 140-foot wall of water, concrete, and debris came rushing down on the unsuspecting residents. It swept through Piru, Fillmore, Santa Paula, and Saticoy as it headed toward the sea, destroying everything in its path, including people, animals, and homes. Estimates of deaths ranged from 400 to 600 people. Bodies washed ashore as far south as San Diego. Thousands of acres of farmland and over 1,000 structures were destroyed. Ten bridges were washed out.

When St. Francis Dam failed, it unleashed a flood that scoured
the canyon all the way to the ocean.
PHOTOGRAPH COURTESY OF THE U.S. GEOLOGICAL SURVEY.

The water moved at an estimated eighteen miles an hour through the first narrow canyon. Few people in the path survived. Powerhouse #2 was swamped by the waters, and flashes in the sky looked like lightning as power lines fell. A few minutes later, the lights in Los Angeles went out, flickered on, and then went dark again. Communications were sporadic, so few residents along the Santa Clara River in Ventura County believed that the dam had actually broken or that the waters posed any danger to them. Some headed for the safety of the hills while a few went to bridges to watch the water come through, not realizing that they too would be swept away.

A 1964 profile on Ray Rising, an employee who worked at Powerhouse #2 below the dam, captured the desperation of being caught in that flood. Rising lost his wife and two daughters to the raging waters that swept down the canyon.

We were all asleep in our wood-framed home in the small canyon just above the powerhouse. I heard a roaring like a cyclone. The water was so high we couldn't get out the front door. The house disintegrated.

Nearly all of the dam washed away except
this remnant nicknamed "the Tombstone" by locals.
PHOTOGRAPH COURTESY OF THE U.S. GEOLOGICAL SURVEY.

In the darkness I became tangled with an oak tree, fought clear, and swam to the surface. I was wrapped with electrical wires and held by the only power pole in the canyon. I grabbed the roof of another house, jumping off when it floated to the hillside. I was stripped of clothing but scrambled up the razorback of a hillside.

Investigations after the fact revealed many attempts to save lives. Two highway patrolmen, Thornton Edwards and Stanley Baker, sped to Santa Paula on their motorcycles with their sirens wailing. Edwards pounded on doors, waking residents in the middle of the night to warn them of the impending danger. He became known as the "Paul Revere of the St. Francis Flood." Local telephone operators, including Louise Gipe in Santa Paula and Reicel Jones in Saticoy, called homes in the water's path. Some residents organized caravans of cars to drive to higher ground. Although the water slowed somewhat by the time it reached Santa Paula, bridges and houses there were still swept away. The Santa Clara River Valley was left in ruins. Rumors flew that the dam had been dynamited, but that was quickly proved false.

The City of Los Angeles took responsibility for the disaster. It placed $1 million in a fund so that the Los Angeles Water and Power Agency

Residents inspect flood damage in Santa Paula.
PHOTOGRAPH COURTESY OF THE U.S. GEOLOGICAL SURVEY.

could settle claims for damages. In addition, men and equipment were sent to provide additional aid. Rather than use the court system to handle the many claims being made, Ventura County set up a committee of local business and government leaders to process them.

The governor appointed a six-member board of inquiry chaired by A. J. Wiley, a consulting engineer from Boise, Idaho. The committee acted fast. The members met a week after the dam failure, made a site visit, and filed their report in Los Angeles on March 27. The board found that the poor quality of the foundation material was the reason the dam failed. The soil and rock weakened as they became saturated with water. This was the same general conclusion reached by most experts who investigated the problem, although there was strong disagreement over the specific details of when, where, and how various parts of the failure occurred.

The governor's board members believed that the dam's right abutment failed first. They based this opinion partly on where various sections of the dam ended up after the breach. Some people complained that the data used by the board were incomplete at the time the report was made. The board was criticized for making only a cursory inspection, for not doing its own measurements, and for relying on faulty data. At least a dozen other reports were later completed by other parties, but they didn't get the publicity of the first published report.

Experts pointed to other factors that might have been involved in the dam failure. Some thought that increasing the height of the dam without increasing its thickness was an error. A number of human factors may also have contributed to the disaster. Warning signs such as cracks and seepage were not heeded, and there was overconfidence in an inexperienced design team. It was also pointed out that California's laws had shortcomings with respect to registration requirements for professional engineers. As a result of the dam failure, the California Legislature immediately enacted changes in the law to elevate the standards.

Los Angeles District Attorney Asa Keyes conducted the coroner's inquest following the disaster. During Mulholland's testimony, those in court watched a home movie of the tragedy. Mulholland, who was clearly tortured by the disaster, sobbed and said, "I envy the dead."

Mulholland took responsibility for the dam's failure. He said, "Don't blame anyone else, you just fasten it on me. If there was an error in human judgment, I was the human."

The coroner's jury deliberated for two weeks and decided that no prosecution was warranted. But the jury did blame Mulholland for lacking the expertise to be the leading authority on such a major dam project. The jury said, "The construction of a municipal dam should never be left to the sole judgment of one man no matter how eminent."

Mulholland and his associates maintained that they didn't suspect a problem and had taken all necessary steps to protect the residents of the area. Questions raised about the choice of the site and the construction of the dam remained unanswered. Ray Rising returned to work at Powerhouse #2 when it was replaced and lived there with a new wife. They raised a family in a home not far from the one that had been swept away.

During the inquest, Mulholland offered to resign, but he was encouraged to stay in his job. Nevertheless, he retired, a broken man, eight months after the disaster and spent his remaining years in seclusion, never recovering from the tragedy. He died of a stroke in 1935 and was buried at Forest Lawn Memorial Park Cemetery in Glendale. The St. Francis Dam was never rebuilt. Today, Los Angeles still receives water from the original aqueduct system, augmented with water from various Northern California rivers and the Colorado River.

In 2018, ninety years after that wall of water rushed down San Francisquito Canyon, Jon Garton, president of the Association of State Dam Safety Officials, said, "The St. Francis Dam failure was a pivotal event in U.S. history in that it forced policymakers to consider their role in ensuring public safety through adequate oversight." Garton also suggested that the best technical knowledge had not been widely disseminated through the engineering community, a challenge that remains today despite ongoing improvements in laws; dam design, operation, and maintenance; and other dam-safety practices.

A Saint Francis Dam Disaster National Memorial and a Saint Francis Dam Disaster National Monument were established by an act of Congress in March 2019. Both areas will be administered by the U.S. Forest Service. The act preserves 353 acres in the Angeles National Forest to commemorate the St. Francis Dam disaster and for the protection of cultural, archaeological, historical, watershed, educational, and recreational resources and values.

SOURCES

Association of State Dam Safety Officials. Dam Failures and Incidents. https://damsafety.org/dam-failures.

Blitz, Matt. "On Occasions Like This, I Envy the Dead: The St. Francis Dam Disaster." *The Smithsonian Magazine*. March 12, 2015.

Burbank, Jeffrey. "Children of the Dammed: On the St. Francis Dam Disaster." *Los Angeles Review of Books*. May 26, 2016.

Harrison, Scott. "California Retrospective: St. Francis Dam collapse left a trail of death and destruction." *Los Angeles Times*. March 19, 2016.

Hundley, Norris, Jr. and Donald C. Jackson. *Heavy Ground: William Mulholland and the St. Francis Dam Disaster*. Oakland, CA: University of California Press and the Huntington Library, 2015.

Jones, Ray and Joe Lublow. *Disasters and Heroic Rescues of California*. Guilford, CT: Globe Pequot Press, 2006.

McWilliams, Carey. *Southern California. An Island on the Land*. Salt Lake City, UT: Gibbs M. Smith, Inc., Peregrine Smith Books, 1973.

Meares, Hadley. "The Flood: St. Francis Dam Disaster, William Mulholland, and the Casualties of L. A. Imperialism." History and Society, KCET. July 26, 2013.

Nichols, John. *St. Francis Dam Disaster*. Images of America, Arcadia Publishing, 2002.

Outland, Charles F. *Man-Made Disaster, The Story of St. Francis Dam, Its Place in Southern California's Water System, Its Failure, and the Tragedy in the Santa*

Clara River Valley, March 12 and 13, 1928. Glendale, CA: The Arthur H. Clark Company, 1977.

Roderick, Kevin. "Dam Disaster Killed 450, Broke Mulholland." *Los Angeles Times*. October 12, 1999.

Roger, J. David. The 1928 St. Francis Dam Failure and Its Impact on American Civil Engineering. For the American Society of Civil Engineers.

Wilkman, Jon. *Floodpath: The Deadliest Man-Made Disaster of 20th-Century America and the Making of Modern Los Angeles*. New York, NY: Bloomsbury Press, 2016.

MONSTER STORMS

TROPICAL CYCLONES ARE SEVERE SEABORNE STORMS THAT DEVELOP over warm water. They're marked by low barometric pressure, strong winds, high waves, and, when they hit land, storm surges. In the Atlantic Ocean north of the equator—in the Caribbean Sea and Gulf of Mexico—these cyclones are called hurricanes, from an indigenous West Indies word that Spanish explorers pronounced *huracan*. In the western Pacific, these storms are known as typhoons, and in the Indian Ocean they're called cyclones. But all such storms are technically tropical cyclones.

In the northern hemisphere, tropical storms and cyclones tend to move from east to west, so they seldom hit the coast of California. Also, tropical cyclones feed on the energy stored in warm ocean water. Due to the influence of the cold coastal California Current from the north and extensive deep upwellings, water temperatures off the California coast rarely get above 70 degrees Fahrenheit. In addition, the upper atmospheric circulation in the subtropical eastern Pacific flows to the west and northwest. This flow usually steers tropical storms off the West Coast of North America and out to sea. Closer to shore, as winds flow off the coast, they have a strong vertical sheer, an effect that weakens ocean storms. So even when storms do form off Central America and head northward, they lose their force when they encounter the cool California Current. In fact, an oceanographer named Bill Patzert calls this current "a hurricane repellent." The few remnants of these storms to reach Southern California are generally harmless.

Three such severe storms have landed direct hits on California: in 1858, 1939, and 1962.

THE 1858 CALIFORNIA HURRICANE

Records from 1858 are understandably sketchy, so accurate information on that year's hurricane is hard to come by. Michael Chenoweth, a hurricane historian, and Christopher Landsea, a science and operations manager at the National Hurricane Center, collected data from the U.S. Coast Survey and U.S. Army sites such as the depot in New San Diego, where weather observations were recorded daily. They also found newspaper accounts of the storm in the *Daily Alta California* and the *Los Angeles Star*. Among the records were two reports from a ship at sea of Force 11 winds and barometric pressure readings of 28.67 inches and 971 millibars. Chenoweth and Landsea classified this as a Category 1 hurricane with winds of 74 to 94 miles per hour. On the morning of October 2, 1858, an official observer in San Diego using a high-quality government barometer reported that the reading was the lowest atmospheric pressure ever recorded in that area.

The *Daily Alta California* newspaper provided a description of the storm from its San Diego-based reporter in its October 3, 1858, edition:

> [T]he whole heavens seemed closing in with bank upon bank of dark, heavy, ominous-looking clouds, fleeting pretty close down to the ground, before the increasing gale. . . . Several very heavy gusts of wind came driving madly along completely filling the atmosphere with thick and impenetrable clouds of dust and sand, so

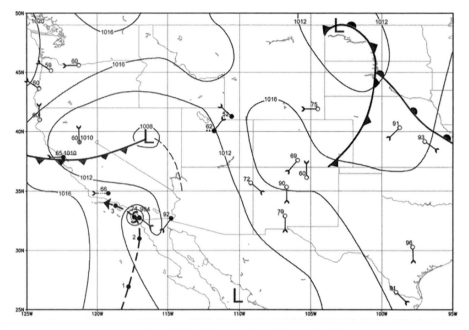

Hurricane researchers Michael Chenoweth and Christopher Landsea created this weather map of the 1858 hurricane based on observations made at the time. MAP COURTESY OF THE NATIONAL OCEANIC AND ATMOSPHERIC ADMINISTRATION.

much so, that one who was in the street could no more see around him than if he was surrounded by an Egyptian darkness. This continued for a considerable length of time, the violence of the wind still increasing until about one o'clock, when it came along in a perfect hurricane, tearing down houses and everything that was in its way. Roofs of houses, trees, fences, etc. filled the air in all directions, doing a large amount of damage, in and about the city and its immediate vicinity. From this time until dark, a continuance of this kind was experienced, interspersed now and then by a crash of house, tree, or something of this kind; with the sun the wind went down, during the night we had a considerable fall of rain which made a very pleasant change. The streets, alleys, and roads, from a distance as far as yet heard from were swept as clean as if a thousand brooms had been laboriously employed for months.

At noon, the gale was so strong at Point Loma that the lighthouse keeper feared the tower would blow away and left his post. The tower withstood the wind, but a windmill recently built at Mission Point was totally destroyed, as were several homes in the area. The schooner *Plutus* dragged its anchor and was blown onto the beach. The schooner *Lovely Flora* was also left high and dry on the beach, and the schooner *X.L.*, under repair at the docks, was blown over.

In addition to the hurricane-strength winds that hit San Diego, the storm brought 39- to 73-mile-per-hour winds along the coast north to Long Beach. When the storm reached San Pedro, the winds did "considerable injury" to small craft anchored in the bay, as well as to a luxury yacht, the *Medora*, which belonged to Phineas Banning, a stagecoach and shipping entrepreneur considered to be "the father of the Port of Los Angeles." A large barge broke up in heavy surf, and a piece of the wharf at San Pedro was swept to sea, along with a considerable amount of lumber stored on shore.

In Los Angeles, the hurricane's heavy rains resulted in flooded streets and homes and the collapse of walls in some adobe buildings. High winds hit El Monte, flattening corn crops. Although some feared grape crops would also be lost, that turned out not to be the case. Farther north, damage from the storm was localized and was unnoticed or barely felt in Santa Barbara and San Luis Obispo, but inland Visalia reported seven inches of rain in one day.

There are no estimates of the costs of the storm damage, but they were likely low because the area was so sparsely populated; Los Angeles had only about 5,000 residents at the time. Chenoweth and Landsea estimated that if such a storm hit today, the damage would likely be more than $500 million dollars.

THE 1939 LONG BEACH TROPICAL STORM

A tropical depression formed off the coast of Central America on September 15, 1939, and began moving west-northwest. Then, reclassified as a hurricane, it turned north-northeast, lost intensity, and became a tropical storm. It passed over Catalina Island and on September 25 hit San Pedro and Long Beach with 72-mile-per-hour gusts. Winds remained at gale force before the storm dispersed later in the day. While not as large or powerful a storm as the 1858 hurricane, this one is notable as the only tropical storm to make landfall in California in the twentieth century. It also brought a high death toll.

The 1939 Long Beach storm is also known as *El Cordonazo*, or the Lash of St. Francis. These latter names are associated with tropical cyclones in the southeastern part of the North Pacific Ocean. Such storms off the coast of Mexico often seem to occur near the feast of St. Francis, celebrated on October 4.

This tropical storm brought heavy rain. Los Angeles received 5.66 inches in twenty-four hours. Mount Wilson received 11.6 inches, while in Indio 7 inches of rain fell during a three-hour thunderstorm. Similar large amounts of rain fell in other nearby cities, such as Raywood Flat and Pasadena. The whole Citrus Belt near Anaheim saw heavy rains. All of this came on top of a rainy period, so the additional rains from the tropical storm caused widespread flooding.

The Hamilton Bowl was designed as a catch basin to hold water until it could flow through storm drains into the Los Angeles River. But the Hamilton Bowl overflowed, flooding the Signal Hill area near Long Beach. The Los Angeles River itself became a raging torrent. Six people caught at the river's mouth on the beach at Long Beach drowned.

Along the shore from Malibu to Huntington Beach, houses were flooded and many people were stranded in their homes. In most areas, electricity and telephone connections were lost. The streets of Los Angeles and Inglewood flooded two to three feet deep, with water pouring into stores and office buildings. Windows were smashed by high winds in Long Beach. In Belmont Shore, waves undercut ten houses and swept them away. Near Indio, rains washed away a 150-foot section of Southern Pacific Railroad track and took out a section of Santa Fe main track near Needles. In the flooded Coachella Valley, growers lost 75 percent of their crops. All told, the flooding killed forty-five people.

At the time, Los Angeles didn't have a government office dedicated to weather forecasting, so the storm caught everyone off guard. (Five months after the storm, such an office was established for Southern California.) The U.S. Coast Guard and Navy were not expecting high winds and heavy seas. An estimated forty-eight to fifty-four people drowned at sea. Some were trying to flee Catalina Island for the mainland. The Coast Guard and Navy conducted many rescue operations, saving the lives of dozens of people. Nevertheless, at least twenty-four people died when a huge wave hit the fishing vessel *Spray* while it was attempting to dock at the Point Mugu pier. The *Spray* was returning from Anacapa Island and was only seventy-five yards offshore when a wave broke over the deck, washing the pilot house full of passengers into the sea. Only two survivors made it to shore. They walked four miles to Oxnard to report the disaster. Another sixteen people from Ventura were killed on a fishing boat named *Lur*. Many other ships were capsized, wrecked, or blown ashore during the storm.

Under the storm-classification system used in 1939, this was considered a tropical storm. At the time, meteorologists doubted that a true hurricane (a violent storm with sustained winds of 74 miles per hour or more) could ever reach California. But in more recent studies, the National Oceanic and Atmospheric Administration determined that such storms, though rare, are a real threat.

Although the Long Beach tropical storm had a 1939-value loss of only $2 million, a similar storm today would be a much more costly disaster. Adjusting for inflation and the area's tremendous population growth, experts estimate that a storm like the 1858 hurricane or the 1939 tropical storm, if it hit today, would cost in the hundreds of millions of dollars.

Data show that surface temperatures in the Pacific Ocean are warming. In the summer of 2018, the ocean temperature off San Diego reached a record

79.5 degrees F., about ten degrees higher than normal and hot enough to feed tropical storms. Many experts agree that when conditions are right, Southern California could experience another disastrous hurricane.

THE BIG BLOW—THE 1962 COLUMBUS DAY STORM

The Columbus Day Storm of October 12, 1962, popularly known as the Big Blow, left vivid memories for many living in California, Oregon, Washington, and British Columbia. Teresa Schomber was in kindergarten in Snoqualmie Falls, Washington, when the storm hit. She and her siblings routinely walked to and from school, but not that day. She remembered that her father came to pick them up. It was pouring rain. Schomber recalled, "The wind was so strong, he carried each kid to the car, one at a time. Because the wind was making us fly."

Fear of being blown away was actually real. Interviewed for a retrospective more than fifty years later, Don Hoyt recollected that his father really did fly. "I remember my neighbor's window breaking out, and me and my dad carried a piece of plywood over to cover the open window, when a burst came up and knocked the neighbor down, and my dad still had hold of the board. The wind picked my dad up off the ground and carried him several feet before he was able to let go. The board went flying and my dad went tumbling like a tumbleweed."

The same storm system had begun hitting the Northern California coast two days earlier with lower winds but all-time record rains. The storm first developed as Typhoon Freda about 500 miles north of Wake Island, in the Pacific Ocean halfway between Hawaii and the Philippines. As it moved north over colder water, Freda lost power and became a low-pressure area, gradually wandering toward the Aleutian Islands and then east toward Northern California. As it neared North America, warm, moist air from the south met very cold air from the north, and the baro-metric pressure dropped to 28.41 inches Hg (962 millibars), creating what is today known as an "atmospheric river." These clashing warm and cold fronts channeled moisture into the San Francisco Bay area beginning on Wednesday, October 10, and then veered sharply north along the coast toward Oregon and Washington. By this time, the storm was equal to a Category 3 hurricane and extended from Northern California to the southern parts of British Columbia.

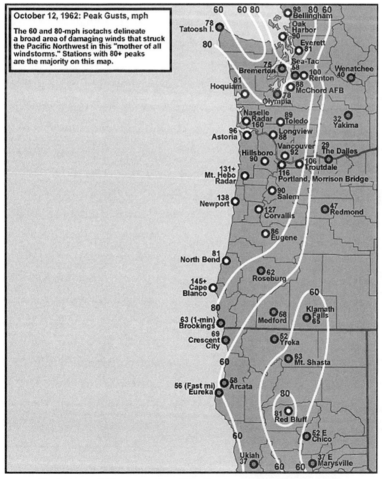

Peak gusts of 80 to more than 130 miles per hour were widespread, with Naselle Radar Station in Washington reporting one blast at 160 miles per hour.
MAP COURTESY OF SPIRITCHASER, CC BY-SA 3.0.

Total damage in the three states ranged from $230 million to $280 million in 1962 dollars. More than sixty people died either directly or indirectly due to the storm. In California, the storm accounted for nineteen deaths. Oregon saw twenty-seven lives lost, Washington eleven, and British Columbia eight. The most common cause of death was getting hit by trees falling on homes and cars. Another 317 people were seriously injured, while hundreds more received minor injuries. This was considered one of the strongest extratropical cyclones ever to make landfall in the United States.

In Oregon and Washington, the storm brought mighty, record-setting winds. Portland documented wind gusts of 116 miles per hour, while at Corvallis, winds were reported at 127 mph before the wind gauge broke and the recorder fled. Gusts as high as 131 mph were recorded at Mount Hebo and 145 mph at Cape Blanco. The winds blew down an estimated 15 million board feet of timber, enough to frame a million houses. Hundreds of miles of power lines also came down, leaving millions of people without electrical power, many for weeks. The storm also damaged orchards and walnut groves and knocked down barns, often crushing or trapping livestock inside. Homes and business buildings throughout much of the Pacific Northwest suffered wind damage.

Winds that hit California, though damaging, were significantly lower. In Red Bluff, winds measured 81 mph, and on Mount Tamalpais just north of San Francisco they measured 80 mph. Requa Air Force Station, on the coast south of Crescent City, recorded gusts of 112 mph.

Buildings were blown apart in Newberg, Oregon, near Portland, during the 1962 Big Blow.
PHOTOGRAPH COURTESY OF THE NATIONAL WEATHER SERVICE.

The winds generated high seas. On Thursday, October 11, about fifty fishing boats left Eureka at Humboldt Bay for their usual fishing day. They ran into fifty-mile-per-hour winds and thirty-foot seas. The U.S. Coast Guard received numerous calls for help from Eureka, Fort Bragg, and San Francisco. Just in time, a Coast Guard cutter from Fort Bragg reached a boat in distress several miles southwest off Eureka and towed it to safety. Another fishing boat, the *Jean Ellen*, sank fifteen miles west of Eureka shortly after two crewmen were rescued by another Coast Guard cutter.

The Big Blow didn't spare inland California. Rainfall amounts were staggering. The community of Ben Lomond in the Santa Cruz Mountains south of San Francisco reported 14.10 inches of rain in twenty-four hours. The waterworks in Orinda, just over the hill from Oakland, received 18.41 inches of rain over two days. Landslides in the Oakland hills destroyed numerous buildings and killed one child.

Observers in Red Bluff reported 0.41 inch of rain in five minutes and 0.98 inch of rain in fifteen minutes. Parts of San Francisco received 7 inches of rain in twenty-four hours. Oakland set an all-time calendar-day record of 4.52 inches of rain on October 13, while Sacramento received 3.77 inches. Due to heavy rains, Game 6 of the World Series between the New York Yankees and the San Francisco Giants, to be held in San Francisco's Candlestick Park, was postponed from October 11 to October 15.

The rains turned the Oakland hills into muddy slopes, forcing hundreds of evacuations and blocking two freeways. On Saturday, a mother and her daughter slid off an embankment in their car and slowly sank in front of onlookers, until the car was completely buried. The driver honked her horn, prompting a successful rescue effort. The two passengers were freed after over an hour of being buried alive. The rescued woman managed to say, "I'm certainly glad to see you," to the rescuers before she fainted.

In the general Bay Area, about 450 homes were destroyed by mudslides and flooding. Forbestown, in Northern California near the Feather River, had the greatest three-day total of any location with 25.78 inches of rain.

In Crescent City, California, half the buildings—both homes and businesses—suffered damage. Some had broken windows, others had damaged roofs and lost television antennas, and many fences were destroyed or blown away. Shasta Lake had six-foot waves. Squaw Creek at Shasta Lake received twelve inches of rain.

The Columbus Day Storm will be long remembered. According to the Metropolitan Life Insurance Company, the Big Blow was the worst national disaster in the United States in 1962. Will it ever be repeated? Kathie Dello, deputy director of Oregon Climate Services at Oregon State University, has said that many factors had to be in place to create the Columbus Day Storm, but by themselves none of these factors was particularly unusual. So it's entirely possible such a storm might come again.

SOURCES

The 1858 California Hurricane

Chenoweth, Michael and Christopher Landsea. "The San Diego Hurricane of 2 October 1858." *American Meteorological Society*. November 2004, pp. 689–697.

Masters, Nathan. "Has a Hurricane Ever Made Landfall in California?" Kcet.org. October 15, 2016.

Sheets, Robert and Jack Williams. *Hurricane Watch: Forecasting the Deadliest Storms on Earth*. Vintage Books, 2001.

The 1939 Long Beach Tropical Storm

1939 California tropical storm. http://enacademic.com/dic.nsf/enwiki/1350453.

Jones, Ken. "Point Mugu Pier—Gone But Not Forgotten." *Pier Fishing in California*. August 24, 2019.

Kalstrom, George W. "El Cordonazo—The Lash of St. Francis." *Weatherwise*. October 1952.

The Big Blow—the 1962 Columbus Day Storm

Burt, Christopher C. "50th Anniversary of the Columbus Day Storm." Weather Underground. October 12, 2012.

Dodge, John. *A Deadly Wind, The 1962 Columbus Day Storm*. Corvallis, OR: Oregon State University Press, 2018.

LaLande, Jeff. "Columbus Day Storm (1962)." *The Oregon Encyclopedia*.

Lucia, Ellis. *The Big Blow*. Portland, OR: Overland Press, 1963.

McLeod, Jaime. "The Columbus Day Storm of 1962." *Farmers' Almanac*. October 2013.

Sistek, Scott. "October 12, 1962: Columbus Day Windstorm Still Ranks as Greatest in the Northwest." KOMO News. October 12, 2017.

AIRPLANE CRASHES

STATISTICALLY, COMMERCIAL PASSENGER FLIGHT IS ONE OF THE SAFEST ways to travel. In 2018 in the United States alone, there were more than 10.3 million scheduled flights carrying a total of more than 1 billion passengers. Commercial flights, including small commuter airlines, average fewer than twenty fatal incidents a year. According to the U.S. Bureau of Transportation Statistics, the number of deaths per passenger mile for flying on commercial airlines is 750 times less than driving a vehicle on the road. Nevertheless, when a plane falls from the sky, the results are often catastrophic.

A CALAMITY OF ERRORS—PSA FLIGHT 182

September 25, 1978, was shaping up to be a frenetic day for California Lieutenant Governor Mervyn Dymally. Realizing just how busy he was going to be, Dymally made a change in plans. Rather than take Pacific Southwest Airlines (PSA) Flight 182 from Sacramento to Los Angeles and San Diego early in the morning, he would fly down the night before. That way he'd be rested and ready for a full day crammed with appointments. Dymally had no idea that this simple change of plans would save his life.

On the fateful morning, PSA Flight 182 left Sacramento, made an uneventful trip to Los Angeles, and departed LAX at about 8:30 A.M. Shortly thereafter, the pilots made contact with San Diego Approach Control, which advised them to land using Runway 27 at Lindbergh Field. They were advised to switch to the Lindbergh Control Tower and follow visual flight rules. The crew of Flight 182 included forty-two-year-old Captain James McFeron, First Officer Robert Fox, Flight Engineer Martin Wahne, and four flight attendants. Off-duty PSA Captain Spencer Nelson was riding in the cockpit's jump seat. The Boeing 727 carried 128 passengers.

It was sunny and clear over San Diego when the controller notified Flight 182 that there was a small Cessna 172 Skyhawk nearby and gave its location. The Cessna had taken off from Montgomery Field, six miles north of San Diego. Aboard were two men, both licensed pilots with commercial flight certificates. Martin Kazy, thirty-two, was instructing David Boswell, who was practicing instrument landing approaches on Runway 9 at Lindbergh Field. Kazy was a certified instrument flight instructor who had logged more than 5,000 flight hours. Boswell, thirty-five, was a U.S. Marine Corps sergeant with 407 flight hours and was working on his instrument rating. As was typical for this kind of practice, Boswell was wearing a hood that limited his peripheral vision and allowed him to look only straight ahead toward the cockpit panel. The men were operating under visual flight rules that didn't require them to file a flight plan. After two runs, the instructor requested a third approach, and the tower gave him permission to do so with instructions to climb toward the northeast.

The controller notified Captain McFeron of the presence of the Cessna and McFeron acknowledged that he saw the plane. According to flight rules, McFeron could continue his approach, but he was required to keep the Cessna in sight at a safe distance and to notify the tower if he lost sight of it. A few minutes later, after turning for the final landing approach, the

Flight 182 crew couldn't see the Cessna. They concluded that it must be behind them, but McFeron never explicitly reported to the controllers that he had lost sight of the small plane. Unknown to the Flight 182 crew, the Cessna had made a right turn to the east, deviating from its assigned northeasterly course. It was now beneath the large plane and on the same course. Possibly adding to the confusion, the yellow fuselage of the Cessna blended with the predominant color of the houses in the residential area beneath the Boeing 727.

Just six weeks earlier, a conflict-alert warning system had been installed at the San Diego approach facility. It was designed to raise an alarm when it sensed an impending collision. In those first weeks of service, it averaged thirteen alarms a day, many of which were false. At 9:01:28 A.M. this alarm went off. Nineteen seconds later the controller told the Cessna pilot that there was traffic in his vicinity. One second later the two planes collided at about 2,600 feet.

There was a loud crunching sound followed by an explosion. The Boeing was about ninety times heavier than the two-seater Cessna beneath it. Observers on the ground later testified that the Boeing banked slightly and the Cessna pitched up. The nose of the Cessna hit the right wing of the Boeing. Fire burst from the damaged wing of the Boeing.

As the jet fell to earth, its right wing was engulfed in flames. The disabled plane banked hard to the right and began a steep, uncontrolled descent. The cockpit voice recorder picked up Captain McFeron saying, "easy baby, easy baby." Six seconds later he radioed air traffic control, saying, "Tower, we're going down, this is PSA." Mere seconds before impact, McFeron radioed "This is it, baby!" and then punched the intercom at 9:02:03, telling passengers to "brace yourself."

Four seconds later, people on the ground heard a loud impact and a mushroom cloud rose into the air; it could be seen for miles. The Boeing 727 had nose-dived into a house in the North Park residential neighborhood at 300 to 400 miles per hour. One of the wings landed in a nearby

PSA Flight 182 banks in the sky over San Diego, out of control and on fire.
PHOTOGRAPH COURTESY OF THE SAN DIEGO AIR AND SPACE MUSEUM.

house, but little of the plane survived the impact. The engines and landing gear were the biggest pieces to survive intact. The Cessna basically disintegrated in the air after the collision. The largest piece from this small plane hit the ground about six blocks away, and more debris scattered throughout the area. Both men aboard the Cessna were killed.

The main impact on the ground was west of Interstate 805, just north of the intersection of Dwight and Nile Streets, northwest of downtown San Diego and Balboa Park. Devastation spread for several blocks. About 60 percent of the entire San Diego Fire Department was immediately dispatched to the scene, and crews began tackling the flames from spilled jet fuel and burning homes. Officials quickly set up a temporary morgue in the gym at nearby St. Augustine High School.

As news of the crash circulated, many San Diegans did what they could to help. At the local blood bank, 1,000 people formed a line around the building seeking to give blood. On learning that there were no survivors and blood wasn't needed, 652 donated blood anyway for use in a future emergency.

All 136 people on board Flight 182 were killed, along with 7 people on the ground. Another 9 people on the ground were injured, and twenty-two homes were damaged or destroyed. At the time, this was the deadliest air disaster in U.S. history. The grim milestone was surpassed just eight months later when American Airlines Flight 191, bound for Los Angeles, crashed on takeoff at O'Hare Airport in Chicago on May 25, 1979, killing all 271 on board and 2 people on the ground.

Investigators from the National Transportation Safety Board had members on the scene in San Diego within twenty-four hours. After weeks of investigation and hearings, the NTSB placed responsibility for the accident on the PSA flight crew, noting their duty to report to air traffic control if they lost visual contact with another airplane. The NTSB report didn't mention the critical fact that the Cessna veered from its route into the path of the PSA jet. The report was adopted by a three-to-one vote.

The dissenting vote was cast by Francis McAdams, a World War II U.S. Navy pilot and attorney who specialized in aviation-related cases. Appointed by President Lyndon Johnson, McAdams had served on the NTSB for twelve years. He wrote a six-page dissent in which he stated that, while the PSA crew was partially responsible for the accident, the air traffic control system was also partially to blame because the "see and avoid" system was outdated and air traffic controllers had ignored the alarm that indicated the planes were on a collision course. McAdams criticized the omission of any mention of the Cessna veering from its assigned course without reporting it to the tower. Despite McAdams' concerns, the position of the NTSB majority prevailed until August 1982, when the board looked at the report once again and this time adopted in total McAdams' dissenting report that spread the blame among the various parties.

As a result of the accident, wrongful-death lawsuits filled the courts for months. Suits were filed against Pacific Southwest Airlines; the federal government, which employed the air traffic controllers; and Gibbs Flite Center, which operated the local flight school that provided the Cessna and employed the instructor, Kazy. Jury selection for the first case began on November 5, 1979, more than a year after the collision. Seventy cases were heard during the next year, and most of those who sued received only a fraction of what they sought. About half of the trials were completed by January 1980, when Pacific Southwest Airlines and the federal government agreed not to dispute their liability. Settlements for survivors were based on each victim's age, profession, earning potential, number of dependents, and other factors.

A memorial plaque honoring those who died in the disaster was placed in the San Diego Aerospace Museum in Balboa Park. In 1998, on the twentieth anniversary of the crash, another plaque was dedicated and a tree was planted near the North Park branch library in memory of the victims.

Incidentally, Mervyn Dymally, whose flight postponement saved his life, later served six years in the California State Assembly. He passed away in 2012 at the age of eighty-six.

DESPAIR IN THE AIR ON FLIGHT 773

Airline disasters aren't always accidents. Sometimes they involve suicide or murder. On May 7, 1964, twenty-seven-year-old Francisco Gonzales bought a ticket on Pacific Airlines Flight 773 from Reno to San Francisco via Stockton. Gonzales lived in San Francisco with his wife and family. Four years earlier, he had been a member of the Philippines Olympic Yachting Team. Now, he worked in a warehouse and was deeply in debt, with half his income going to loan payments. He was depressed and angry. More than once he had threatened to kill his family and others. He told relatives and friends that he was going to die on May 6 or 7.

On the evening of May 6, Gonzales bought a Smith and Wesson .357 magnum. Then he went to the airport, where he bought two life insurance policies worth more than $100,000 dollars combined; he named his wife as the beneficiary. He flew to Reno, where he spent the night gambling.

Early the next morning, Gonzales boarded his flight home. At that time there were no X-ray machines or security checks of passengers. He boarded Pacific Airlines Flight 773 carrying the gun.

The airplane was a Fairchild F-27 twin-turboprop with a cargo hold between the cockpit and the passenger section. There were thirty-three passengers and three crew members, including Captain Ernest Clark, fifty-two, and First Officer Ray Andress, thirty-one. The plane landed in Stockton at 6:30 A.M. Two passengers left the plane and ten new passengers boarded, bringing the total on board (crew and passengers) to forty-four.

The plane took off for the twenty-minute flight to San Francisco at 6:38 A.M. After ten minutes, the captain began his descent. Gonzales quickly moved to the cockpit, where he shot and killed Clark and wounded Andress. Andress tried to fly the plane and somehow managed to radio air traffic controllers, saying, "PAL 773, Skipper's shot. . . we've been shot . . . trying to help. . . ." Then the plane vanished from radar. Another aircraft nearby reported a black cloud of smoke rising through the low clouds and gave its location. Searchers soon found the crash site on a hillside near San Ramon in Contra Costa County. There were no survivors.

Thirty-six people were killed when Pacific Air Flight 773 crashed near San Ramon.
PHOTOGRAPH COURTESY OF THE FEDERAL AVIATION ADMINISTRATION.

Observers said the plane nose-dived into the ground. Investigators discovered the gun with six spent cartridges. They found that the plane had been set to fly level, so they speculated that Gonzales himself forced the plane into its final nosedive.

MURDEROUS REVENGE AT 26,000 FEET ABOARD FLIGHT 1771

A theft of $69 worth of in-flight cocktail receipts in the Los Angeles airport terminal led to murder and another plane crash in December 1987. David A. Burke, an aircraft cleaning specialist with USAir, confessed to stealing the money. The event had been caught on a hidden camera. At an appeal hearing on December 7, his request for leniency was denied. His supervisor, Raymond Thomson, fired him.

After the firing, Burke was very angry and moody. He left a message on a telephone answering machine to his estranged girlfriend in Los Angeles, saying, "Jackie, this is David. I am on my way to San Francisco, Flight 1771. I love you; I really wish I could say more, but I do love you."

The supervisor, Thomson, commuted to Los Angeles each day from his home in the San Francisco area. After work on this day, he boarded Pacific Southwest Airlines (PSA) Flight 1771, a British Aerospace commuter jet, for the trip home as usual. Burke, carrying a .44 magnum pistol, used his USAir employee identification badge to avoid going through metal detectors and boarded the same flight. (USAir had recently acquired PSA but operated the airline under its old name.) After takeoff, Burke removed an air-sickness bag from the seat pocket and wrote a note on it: "Hi, Ray. I think it's sort of ironical that we end up like this. I asked for some leniency for my family. Remember? Well, I got none and you'll get none." Investigators believed that Burke dropped this note in Thomson's lap about halfway to San Francisco. Shortly thereafter, as the aircraft cruised at 26,000 feet above the central California coast, Burke shot Thomson twice. At the time the plane's captain, Gregg Lindamood, and first officer, James Nunn, were speaking with air traffic control about some turbulence, and the cockpit voice recorder picked up the sound of two gunshots.

Captain Lindamood reported hearing gunfire to the tower. The voice recorder later found in the wreckage of the plane told the story of what happened next. A woman's voice (presumably flight attendant Deborah Neil) was recorded saying, "We have a problem." Lindamood asked, "What kind of problem?" And then Burke replied, "I am the problem." There were two more shots. Then a final shot was heard. No one can be sure, but investigators speculated that this was when Burke shot another pilot who was on board as a passenger: Douglas Arthur, Pacific Southwest Airlines' chief pilot in Los Angeles. It's possible that Arthur ran to the cockpit to stop Burke, or perhaps Burke shot himself.

After nose-diving from 26,000 feet, the airplane smashed into a rocky hillside at a cattle ranch between Paso Robles and Cayucos. The plane hit the ground going 770 miles per hour. All thirty-eight passengers and five crew members were killed. Crash-scene investigators found a gun with a piece of finger attached. The flesh was that of David Burke. They also found six used cartridges and the note that Burke had written to Thomson.

As a result of this crash, the Federal Aviation Administration changed its rules to require everyone, including airline and airport employees, to undergo screening for weapons. Airline companies immediately began confiscating all airline and airport employee credentials whenever an employee was terminated from his or her job.

The crash of Flight 1771 also affected travel policies for many major U.S. companies. Several company executives had been on board the flight, including James Sylla, president of Chevron USA, and three Chevron public-affairs executives: Owen Murphy, Jocelyn Kempe, and

Allen Swanson. Three officials with Pacific Bell, a telephone company, were also killed in the crash. Afterward, many companies prohibited multiple executives from traveling on the same flight.

SOURCES

A Calamity of Errors—PSA Flight 182

Aircraft Accident Report: Pacific Southwest Airlines, Inc., B-727, N533PS and Gibbs Flite Center, Inc., Cessna 172, N7711G San Diego, California, September 25, 1978. National Transportation Safety Board. April 20, 1979.

Bevil, Alexander D. "'Memories that will never go away': The crash of flight 182 and its aftermath." *The Journal of San Diego History*. Spring 2017, Volume 63, Number 3+4.

Hall, Matthew T. "Crash of PSA Flight 182 vivid 35 years later." *The San Diego Union-Tribune*. September 25, 2013.

Monteagudo, Merrie. "From the Archives: September 25, 1978: The Crash of PSA Flight 182." *The San Diego Union-Tribune*. September 25, 2020.

Serling, Robert J. *Loud and Clear: The Full Answer to Aviation's Vital Question—Are the Jets Really Safe?* Doubleday & Co., 1969.

Despair in the Air on Flight 773

Aviation Safety Network. Pacific Flight 773 database record. Flight Safety Foundation.

Civil Aeronautics Board. *Aircraft Accident Report: Pacific Air Lines, Inc. Fairchild F-27, N277OR Near San Ramon, California, May 7, 1964*. Released November 2, 1964.

Murderous Revenge at 26,000 Feet Aboard Flight 1771

Associated Press. "Fired worker's death note to ex-boss found." *The Spokesman-Review*. December 11, 1987.

Fisher, Lawrence. "4 Chevron Officials Died in Air Crash." *The New York Times*. December 9, 1987.

Jones, Ray and Joe Lubow. *Disasters and Heroic Rescues of California*. Guilford, CT: Globe Pequot Press, 2006.

King, Peter and Eric Malnic. "Crash of Pacific Southwest Airlines jetliner centers on fired employee." *Los Angeles Times*. December 9, 1987.

Magnuson, Ed. "David Burke's Deadly Revenge." *Time Magazine*. Sunday, June 24, 2001.

Malnic, Eric. "PSA crash liability case may hinge on airport security." *Los Angeles Times*. June 5, 1989.

Pollack, Andrew. "California Plane Crash Kills 44; Gunshots are Reported in Cabin." *The New York Times*. December 8, 1987.

SHARK ATTACKS

MAKE AND MAINTAIN EYE CONTACT WITH A SHARK? THAT'S WHAT ONE expert suggests if you encounter a shark while swimming. Since sharks are ambush predators, they supposedly won't attack their prey if they know they've been spotted. The same expert warns not to wear a shiny or glittery swimsuit because it might look too much like fish scales and tempt a shark. Her final piece of advice is that, if you're attacked, you should fight back and kick at the shark.

The International Shark Attack File shows that between 1958 and 2016 there were 2,785 confirmed, unprovoked shark attacks around the world. Of these, 439 were fatal. The United States saw the most attacks of any nation, with 1,105. Australia ranked second with 536 attacks. In 2015, there were 98 unprovoked attacks worldwide, which is the highest annual total ever recorded. Slightly more than half of these were attacks on surfers. These numbers may be considerably lower than the actual number of attacks since many coastal countries don't report or publicize such incidents.

According to an annual survey compiled by the International Shark Attack File at the Florida Museum, California ranks fourth in the nation in the number of shark attacks. Other reports rank it third. Hawaii and

Florida typically see more attacks, while Texas has about the same number as California. Among California counties, San Diego County has had the greatest number of shark attacks since 1926, but attacks occur all along the California coast. An unnerving number of these are by great white sharks. Cindy Michaels, director of communications for Shark Diver, a California-based tour company, provided an explanation for the presence of great white sharks in the state's coastal waters. According to her, the sharks "go up and down the whole coast of California to the Farallon Islands in San Francisco; that's where they're mating, they're pupping, they're swimming around looking for food." It's also the case that in summer, warm water brings schools of fish closer to shore where people are, and that's where sharks come to feed.

According to the California Department of Fish and Wildlife, there have been 184 shark attacks off the state's coast since 1950, and 13 of them were fatal. At least 163 of the attacks involved great white sharks, including all of the fatal ones. Scientists believe that this species of shark has been around for 16 million years and can be found in every ocean in the world.

Sharks' only enemies are orcas and humans. Great whites are four to five feet long at birth, but they can grow up to twenty feet long and weigh up to 5,000 pounds. Despite their size, they can cruise along at about five miles per hour and can reach speeds of up to twenty-five miles per hour or more in short bursts. Recent research indicates that great whites may live seventy years or more. Most of the sharks along the Southern California coast are juveniles, usually ranging from six to ten feet in length. They catch fish and stingrays in these warmer waters, especially in summer. When they're bigger they tend to move farther north into cooler waters, where they prey on seals and sea lions.

Great white sharks have a torpedo-shaped body and are charcoal-gray to gray-brown or black on top and white below, with a sharp but some-what ragged demarcation between the two colors. They have a narrow tail stalk and a crescent-shaped tail. Their eyes are relatively large and dark.

Great white sharks frequent the waters off the coast of California.
PHOTOGRAPH BY TERRY GOSS, CC BY-SA 2.5.

Their pectoral fins have white edges and the tips underneath are black. Some individuals also have a black spot beneath their pectoral fins.

The triangular-shaped teeth of great whites are long and serrated. The teeth aren't fixed in sockets; instead their roots are implanted in the connective tissue of the jaw. That makes it easy for a tooth to break off and lodge in the shark's prey. During its lifetime, a great white may shed as many as 30,000 teeth, but replacement teeth form in rows behind the current teeth. Each shark jaw has five or more rows of teeth. As front teeth are lost, replacement teeth take their place. This continues throughout the animal's life.

Shark experts have identified certain areas along the Southern California coast where juvenile sharks are frequently found in summer. Between 2008 and 2011, the spot most favored by these sharks was Will Rogers Beach off the Palisades. From 2011 to 2014, it was Manhattan Beach. More recently, a favorite spot was Capistrano Beach. The hot spot for sharks moves slightly from year to year.

SEA KAYAKING NEAR MALIBU

Although shark attacks are fairly rare, when they do occur they're dramatic. Roy Stoddard and Tamara McAllister went kayaking together on January 26, 1989, near Malibu in Los Angeles County. Both were graduate students in public health and worked part-time at the University of California-Los Angeles. The couple were in almost daily training for a triathlon they were planning to enter. They often made the three- to four-mile round-trip from Latigo Point to Paradise Cove.

On this particular morning, they were observed launching their kayaks at about 9:30 A.M. More than an hour later, a resident of Paradise Cove reported seeing roiling and thrashing in the water out beyond the kelp beds, west and south of the U.S. Coast Guard buoy. The witness reported that the disturbance went on for five or ten minutes and then all was calm again. Seals that frequently swam near the buoy were observed there at this time, and they appeared agitated.

On January 27, two kayaks were found upside down and lashed together a little less than four miles off nearby Zuma Beach. They were towed to the Channel Island Harbor in Oxnard. Then, on the afternoon of Saturday, January 28, Tamara McAllister's body was found by a sailboat crew about six miles from the Channel Islands. She was wearing a zipped windbreaker jacket over a bathing suit. A week-long search using two boats and a helicopter was started for Roy Stoddard, but no sign of him was ever found.

Various experts studied the evidence to try to reconstruct what had happened. Kayaks are commonly lashed together when paddlers stop to swim or rest. Since McAllister was wearing a jacket, it didn't appear likely that the pair had stopped to swim. If a wind comes up and the water is choppy, paddling kayaks can become difficult. Perhaps the two kayaks were lashed together with Stoddard in front to make it easier for McAllister to paddle.

The condition of the kayaks indicated that a great white shark attacked them from beneath. McAllister was thrown backward out of her kayak, while Stoddard was probably thrown forward, perhaps striking his head on one of the kayaks. Warren Lovell, the Ventura County coroner, submitted a report that read, "Tamara McAllister died from exsanguination [blood loss], the result of massive tissue loss to the upper left thigh and a traumatic wound to the upper right thigh that severed the femoral artery and vein. Measurement of the left thigh injury exceeded 34 cm [13.4 inches] in diameter." The dimension of the wound suggested that it was inflicted by a great white about sixteen feet long.

SWIMMING WITH PREY— AVILA BEACH SHARK ATTACK

On August 19, 2003, a lone swimmer was attacked at Avila Beach, a small community on the north end of San Luis Obispo Bay about 170 miles north of Los Angeles. Fifty-year-old Deborah Franzman, a teacher of philosophy and ethics at Allan Hancock College in nearby Santa Maria, was a regular visitor to the beach. She swam there three or four times a week, usually with friends. On this morning she was alone, wearing a wet suit and fins and swimming with a group of sea lions in water about twenty feet deep. Sea lions are common prey of great white sharks. Franzman was about 200 yards south of the Avila Beach pier and 75 yards from shore, within view of people on the pier and beach, where about thirty lifeguards were training. She was well within the swimming boundary. According to witnesses, at 8:15 A.M., a great white shark estimated to be twelve to sixteen feet long attacked from below, tearing tissue from Franzman's left thigh.

Five of the lifeguards hurried to help. One borrowed a cell phone from a passerby to call 911. The other four leaped into the water, dragged Franzman to shore, and tried to stop the bleeding. They performed cardiopulmonary resuscitation, but paramedics pronounced her dead at the scene. She left behind a partner and a teenage son.

SPEARFISHING NEAR PEBBLE BEACH

On November 24, 2017, twenty-five-year-old Grigor Azatian went spear-fishing with his father, Armen, off Pebble Beach, California. Grigor, a computer-science student at the University of California-Irvine, had already caught a few fish. He'd fished in this area before and was experienced in diving and spearfishing. At one point, Grigor put his speargun back in his Zodiac-style boat and grabbed an underwater camera instead. He took photographs for about twenty minutes and then returned to the boat, swapped back to his speargun, and dove to the bottom, where he found no fish. He surfaced and then made another dive, spotting nothing of interest. But then, on his way back to the surface, he spied a great white shark swimming toward his boat.

Within seconds after Grigor broke the surface, the shark attacked him. It bit him on the right leg and turned him onto his back. Grigor began lashing out with both arms, and he thought he hit the shark with his left hand. He'd dropped his spear, and the knife he always carried was strapped to his leg where the shark was biting. Finally, the shark released its grip and

Grigor swam for his boat as fast as he could. Once on the boat, he looked for his father. Armen, a doctor, was swimming toward the boat. He climbed on board and tried to stop the bleeding from his son's right leg by fashioning a rope into a tourniquet. There was a lot of blood in the boat,

Due to their size and large, razor-sharp teeth, great white sharks can inflict a devastating bite.
PHOTOGRAPH BY OLGA ERNST, CC BY-SA 4.0.

but Armen thought it unlikely that a major artery had been cut. Both men tried to summon help using their cell phones, but neither phone was working properly. Armen cut the anchor on their boat and began to row as fast as he could toward the pier in Stillwater Cove.

When they reached the pier, Armen yelled to some fishermen to call 911, but a house painter who had heard Grigor screaming had already called emergency services. Two off-duty deputies who had been fishing nearby met Grigor at the beach and were joined by another officer who had been dispatched. They applied two tourniquets to Grigor's wounds. About five minutes later, paramedics rushed Grigor to the hospital. The wounds revealed that the shark bit at least twice and maybe three times and that one of its bites may have been deflected by a lead weight that Grigor was wearing. Though his wounds were serious, Grigor Azatian made a complete recovery.

DIVING FOR LOBSTER OFF ENCINITAS

ON SATURDAY, SEPTEMBER 30, 2018, JUST BEFORE 7 A.M., A SHARK attacked a thirteen-year-old boy, Keane Webre-Hayes, who was diving for lobster at Leucadia State Beach (also known as Beacon's Beach) in Encinitas. It was just one hour into opening day of the lobster-diving season. The attack occurred 115 feet offshore in about 9 feet of water. When bitten, the boy began to scream and attracted the attention of three other lobster divers. One man who was kayaking nearby heard the screams and went to the boy's rescue, as did lifeguards and several other swimmers. By that time there was a stream of blood trailing behind Webre-Hayes.

The men pulled the boy onto the kayak and hurried to shore. One of the men later said that the shark followed the kayak. "He didn't want to give up yet," said the man. Once ashore, a rescue crew loaded Webre-Hayes onto a helicopter that took him to Rady Children's Hospital in San Diego; he was admitted in critical condition. He had a deep bite around his left clavicle that went through the muscles to the chest wall. He required more than 1,000 stitches to his face, neck, ear, and left side. Amazingly, Webre-Hayes made a good recovery and eventually returned to school. "He's very brave, very strong, athletic. He's a warrior," said his mother. She said her son was eager to return to playing baseball and getting back in the ocean. Webre-Hayes said that when he was first attacked, he thought one of his buddies was playing with him. The shark that bit him was eventually identified through DNA analysis as a great white.

SURFING AT MONTANA DE ORO STATE PARK

In January 2019, Nick Wepner, a nineteen-year-old surfer and student at California Polytechnic State University in San Louis Obispo, was bitten by a shark off Montana de Oro State Park on California's central coast about 200 miles northwest of Los Angeles. The great white shark, estimated to be fifteen feet long, swam up from beneath him and bit him in the ankle and thigh. Wepner later reported that he kicked the shark and it swam away. A clear set of teeth marks was left on his surfboard. Wepner thought that the unpleasant taste of foam and fiberglass might have encouraged the shark to swim away and leave him alone. Actually, shark researchers worldwide have reported finding some extremely unlikely things in the stomachs of great whites, including a raincoat, boots, baskets, two pumpkins, a cat, a dog, a goat, and a car license plate.

Wepner, an experienced surfer and trained lifeguard, paddled to shore, where a friend helped him to a car and drove him to the hospital. His leg wounds needed fifty stitches. The park manager posted a shark-attack warning on a thirteen-mile stretch of the beach. Although warned of the danger, surfers could—and did—still go into the water.

SAND DOLLAR BEACH TRAGEDY

As this book was being prepared for publication, another Californian lost his life to a shark. At about 1:30 P.M. on Saturday, May 9, 2020, Ben Kelly, twenty-six years old and a respected surfboard maker based in Watsonville and Santa Cruz, was bitten while surfing off Sand Dollar Beach, about one mile south of Manresa State Beach toward the northern end of Monterey Bay. Kelly was 100 yards offshore and in the company of two fellow surfers. Witnesses notified emergency services, but when paramedics arrived, Kelly was dead. He had bled out from a leg wound. At this time, the species of shark that attacked Kelly remains unknown. In the weeks before the attack, a drone pilot had captured video of dozens of large sharks near shore in the northern end of the bay.

Can you protect yourself from shark attacks? Experts remind people that shark attacks are extremely rare, but you can minimize your risk by following these guidelines: always swim at designated and patrolled beaches; leave the water immediately if a shark is spotted in the vicinity; don't swim alone or far from shore; avoid swimming at dawn, dusk, or night; and finally, avoid swimming where seals or sea lions congregate or near schools of fish.

SOURCES

De Maddalena, Alessandro. *Sharks: The Perfect Predators*. Auckland Park, South Africa: Jacana Media (Pty) Ltd., 2008.

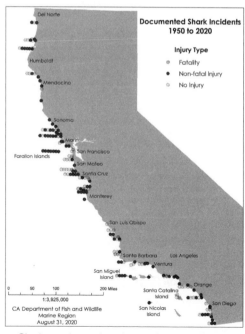

Shark attacks tend to cluster where more people (not necessarily more sharks) are in the water.
MAP COURTESY OF THE CALIFORNIA DEPARTMENT OF FISH AND WILDLIFE.

Domeier, Michael L., ed. *Global Perspectives on the Biology and Life History of the White Shark*. Boca Raton, FL: CRF Press, 2012.

Pierson, Dashel. "Shark Migration in Southern California." *Surfline*. April 13, 2018.

Sea Kayaking Near Malibu

Sharkbait. 1989/01/26 Tamara McAllister – California ***Fatal***. Shark Attack Survivors. September 21, 2008. sharkattacksurvivors.com/shark_attack/viewtopic.php?t=1150

Swimming with Prey—Avila Beach Shark Attack

Guara, Maria Alcia and Chuck Squatriglia. "Shark kills woman in central coast attack." SFGate. August 20, 2003.

Spearfishing Near Pebble Beach

McMurray, Kevin. "Interview with California great white shark attack survivor Grigor Azatian." *Tracking Sharks*. April 25, 2018.

Diving for Lobster Off Encinitas

Garcia, Sandra E. "Shark Attacks a Teenager Diving for Lobsters off the California Coast." *The New York Times*. September 30, 2018.

"'Ten feet of blood': kayaker recalls helping teen attacked by shark in California." CBS News. October 1, 2018.

Surfing at Montana de Oro State Park

"Great white shark attacks surfer." CBS News. January 10, 2019.

Sand Dollar Beach Tragedy

"Fatal Shark Attack Victim Identified as Santa Cruz Surfer Ben Kelly," CBS SF. May 9, 2020.

Ting, Eric. "Surfer killed in shark attack at Santa Cruz County Beach," SFGate. May 10, 2020.

TRAIN WRECKS

DURING THE MID-1800S, ONLY A FEW SCATTERED LOCAL RAIL LINES—
notably the Arcata and Mad River Railroad and the Sacramento Valley
Railroad—provided service in California. But the completion of the first
transcontinental line in 1869 ushered in a new era of travel by rail.

Today, throughout the United States, passenger rail is one of the safest
ways to travel, second only to commercial airline flight. Rail accidents are
rare, and most fatalities associated with rail traffic aren't passengers but
pedestrians and motorists struck by trains.

This chapter highlights four train accidents in California that ably
demonstrate the role human error too often plays in such catastrophes.
As befits the statistical trends mentioned above, three of these accidents
involved freight trains. The fourth centered on a commuter train that
collided with a local freighter.

SAN BERNARDINO TRAIN WRECK, 1989

About thirty miles north of San Bernardino, Interstate 15 and Historic
Route 66 thread between the San Bernardino and San Gabriel Mountains
through a narrow gap known as Cajon Pass, 3,777 feet above sea level.
Several sets of railroad tracks also wind over the pass, and the descent into

the San Bernardino Valley follows one of the steepest railroad grades in the United States, at 3 percent. (In the United States, a grade of 2.5 percent is considered the upper limit for railroads.) The tracks are busy mostly with freight trains, but Amtrak's *Southwest Chief* also provides daily passenger service over Cajon Pass on its run between Los Angeles and Chicago. Given the combination of steep grades and frequent train traffic, it's no surprise that the area has seen its share of wrecks.

Early on the morning of Friday, May 12, 1989, residents on Duffy Street in the Muscoy neighborhood of northwest San Bernardino were getting ready to go to work and send their children off to school. Suddenly, at 7:36 A.M., the ground began to shake and a rumble rippled through the air. Early David, fifty-six, had just picked up her morning newspaper and was sitting on her front porch. She thought it was an earthquake and shouted, "It's here! It's here! The big one!"

In fact, the shaking and rumbling were from a runaway train descending from Cajon Pass. The Southern Pacific Extra 7551 East had just come off the rails at 100 miles per hour and plowed into the homes lining Duffy Street.

The train included sixty-nine hopper cars filled with the mineral trona, as well as four locomotives at the front and two helper locomotives at the rear. The trona—which is used to manufacture glass, paper, detergents, and textiles—was from an Owens Lake mining company that had contracted with Southern Pacific for sixty-nine cars at 100 tons per car. That was the amount loaded onto each car, but when the weight was estimated for the shipper's bill of lading it was listed as 60 tons per car. As a result, when the chief railroad dispatcher calculated the weight for all sixty-nine cars together, he underestimated the total tonnage by almost 3,000 tons. Too few locomotives were used to control the train's descent from Cajon Pass.

To make matters worse, the dynamic brakes on one of the helper engines weren't working. Most trains are equipped with two brake systems: dynamic brakes, which use an electric traction motor to slow the locomotive, and air brakes, which supply braking to each car through a series of pipes and hoses. Both braking systems can be used to control a train's speed, particularly when descending a steep grade.

As Extra 7551 East rolled down the west side of Cajon Pass, it gradually gained speed. The head-end engineer, thirty-three-year-old Frank Holland, used both the dynamic and air brakes to control the 3,470-foot-long train, but each time he did so the train soon accelerated again. By milepost 447, Holland had used all of the train's braking capacity, but the train continued to gain speed. At that point, at the train's rear, the helper engineer, forty-two-year-old Lawrence Hill, realized that their speed was beyond control. He applied the emergency brakes, which rely on the air brakes and automatically deactivate the dynamic brakes. Still the train barreled on, gaining speed.

A woman driving to work on a nearby highway noticed that the train was "going a lot faster than some I had normally seen before." She also saw blue smoke coming from beneath the train—the brakes had overheated. When head-end engineer Holland looked back over the train, he too saw that it was engulfed in smoke. He told the conductor, "Get on the phone and tell them we got a runaway train." The conductor did so, but he downplayed the situation, saying, "We have a slight problem. I don't know if we can get this train stopped."

Helper engineer Hill heard this radio message and immediately issued his own: "Mayday! Mayday! 7551 . . . we're doing 90 miles per hour, nine-zero, out of control." He then got on the floor and braced himself against the locomotive's control panel.

At milepost 486.6, the galloping train approached the elevated Muscoy curve, which had a maximum authorized speed of thirty-five miles per hour. Frank Holland later testified that "[t]he speedometer only went up to 80 [miles per hour], but it was way past that. . . . [the needle] was as far as it could go." The train leapt off the rails and down the embankment into the Duffy Street neighborhood.

Trona blankets the scene where Extra 7551 careened
off the tracks into the Duffy Street neighborhood.
PHOTOGRAPH BY JEREMY A. GREENE, CC BY-SA 4.0.

At that moment, two San Bernardino police officers were driving toward an overpass that spanned the railroad tracks nearby. They saw a big flash and a billowing dust cloud. They radioed dispatch to report the derailed train and request a full emergency response. Then they parked their patrol car and ran up the tracks toward the wreck. Two gas company employees also happened to see the derailment and rushed to the scene. They helped pull Holland, injured but alive, from the lead locomotive. The conductor, thirty-five-year-old Everett Crown, was dead, crushed in the same locomotive. The gas employees went from house to house shutting off gas lines in case any were damaged and leaking before they could ignite.

Seven houses were completely destroyed and four others were extensively damaged. Eight people were at home at the time of the accident. Two young boys—stepbrothers Jason Thompson, seven, and Tyson White, nine—were killed in one of the houses, crushed by the derailed train. Another resident, twenty-four-year-old Chris Shaw, survived after being trapped under debris for fifteen hours. A rescue coordinator remarked, "I would never have believed that this individual could have survived. He had major train parts against his body." Shaw had been dozing in bed when the train demolished his home. Parts of the train had barely avoided crushing him to death and had, in fact, saved his life by forming an air pocket around him and preventing him from suffocating beneath tons of sand-like trona. Debris was piled twenty-five feet high where Shaw's home had been. Rescuers had to dig by hand to carefully remove him from the wreckage. Shaw was sent to San Bernardino County Hospital in serious condition with a fractured pelvis, broken right leg, and other injuries.

Local officials briefly evacuated other homes in the area over concern that the derailment might have damaged a high-pressure gasoline pipeline operated by Calnev. The pipe was buried just four to eight feet underground and paralleled the railroad tracks. After finding no signs of damage to the pipeline, Calnev eventually allowed residents with undamaged houses to return home.

All four of the locomotives at the front of the train were destroyed. All sixty-nine hopper cars were destroyed and were scrapped on-site.

Holland survived with broken ribs and a punctured lung. Helper engineer Lawrence Hill and brakeman Robert Waterbury both suffered only minor injuries. Remarkably, of the train's five-man crew, only the conductor, Crown, and the front brakeman, forty-three-year-old Allan Riess, were killed in the wreck.

As bad as all this was, more trouble was yet to come. Immediately after the train wreck, cleanup crews with bulldozers cleared and repaired the track. After the locomotives and hopper cars were taken away, an excavator

Derailed cars and spilled trona nearly buried this home on Duffy Street.
PHOTOGRAPH BY JEREMY A. GREENE, CC BY-SA 4.0.

removed the spilled trona. Four days after the accident, service on that portion of the train track was restored. But remember the underground Calnev pipeline? During the cleanup, Calnev teams marked its location with spray paint and stakes and monitored all heavy-equipment activity to ensure the pipeline's integrity. Calnev also excavated along the pipeline with backhoes and hand shovels to inspect it. The pipeline appeared to be intact, although when Calnev tried to shut off valves on either side of the derailment area, the company couldn't confirm that the valves worked properly.

Thirteen days later, on May 25, shortly after a train navigated the Muscoy curve at about 8 A.M., the pipeline burst. At high pressure, a plume of vaporized gasoline sprayed into the sky and drifted down onto the houses below. At 8:05 A.M., the gasoline ignited, probably from a gas pilot light in one of the homes. Flames shot hundreds of feet into the air, and an estimated 300,000 gallons of burning gasoline coated the neighborhood.

Emergency crews once again rushed to Duffy Street, but the fire burned for seven hours. Only one house hadn't been damaged on the railroad side of the street during the derailment, but it burned to the ground in the pipeline fire. Two people burned to death, three others were seriously injured, and sixteen more residents suffered minor injuries. The fire consumed eleven houses, and six others received fire or smoke damage. Twenty-one automobiles were destroyed. Total damages from the train derailment and the pipeline rupture and fire exceeded $14 million, most of it due to the fire.

Calnev repaired the pipeline, buried it six feet deep, and encased it in concrete. Not satisfied, residents of the Duffy Street neighborhood tried to have the pipeline closed. A superior court judge heard the case and said he lacked jurisdiction to close the pipeline. A few years later, the pipeline was sold to Kinder Morgan Energy Partners. They actually increased the number of barrels of fuel pumped through the pipe each day.

Many residents received settlements from Calnev and Southern Pacific Railroad, but one attorney representing victims reportedly took settlement money and fled to Spain. The city rezoned the lots on Duffy Street closest to the train tracks as open space. City officials and the pipeline company promised to turn the area into a landscaped greenbelt with an irrigation system, but vandals destroyed the irrigation system and the city park system no longer keeps the greenbelt area going. It's now just a vacant weedy lot. Just a few miles north of the accident site, employees of the Southern Pacific Railroad placed a white cross, a marble bench, and a plaque to commemorate the trainmen who had lost their lives in this accident.

People who live on Duffy Street today say that nothing much has changed since this disaster. They live in fear and their houses still shake as the freight trains rumble past.

DUNSMUIR TRAIN DERAILMENT AND TOXIC SPILL, 1991

Sometimes, "natural" disasters stem from unnatural ingredients. Such is the case when toxic materials are unintentionally released into a healthy ecosystem. One such toxin is metam sodium, also known as carbam, an organosulfur compound that's deadly to plants, animals, and fungi. Because it's lethal to so many plants and organisms, metam sodium is one of the most widely used agricultural pesticides and herbicides on the market. From farms to golf courses, it's applied to the soil to control weeds, fungi, insects, and other pests.

Needless to say, dumping a railcar full of metam sodium into a clean mountain river would be catastrophic for everything living in it. Every safeguard should be in place to ensure that such a calamity never happens. But these ingredients—toxins, a pristine environment teeming with life, and human misstep—read like a recipe for Murphy's Law. So it was when something that could go wrong did go very wrong on the night of Sunday, July 14, 1991, about fifty miles north of Redding in the Trinity Mountains near Mount Shasta.

At the time, the Upper Sacramento River was one of California's most popular trout streams, a blue-ribbon fishery that attracted anglers from around the world. Those visitors were the economic lifeblood of local towns, including Dunsmuir, where the river coursed clear and clean through the eastside neighborhoods, and the official slogan was "Home of the best water on Earth." It was midsummer, the height of the fishing season, and the river was full of young fish from the spring spawning runs.

All that abruptly changed at 9:50 P.M. that Sunday. A Southern Pacific train bound from Colton, California, to Eugene, Oregon, was chugging north up the river canyon just upstream from Dunsmuir. The train included seven locomotives—four in front and three pushing from the rear—and ninety-seven cars: six heavy gondola cars filled with scrap metal at the rear, eighty-four empty cars, a tanker car, and then six more empty cars. The train was crewed by just two men—an engineer and a conductor.

To navigate the steep grade, the tracks switchback across and above the river through two tight horseshoe bends. At the first of these, known as Cantara Loop, a short bridge spans the river. At this bridge, the fourth locomotive derailed, dragging the following seven cars with it. Two of those cars, including the tanker, fell down the embankment and into the river. They landed in about two feet of water. The conductor quickly checked the manifest to determine whether the tanker's contents were listed as hazardous. He found nothing to warrant concern, so he and the engineer walked back to the derailed cars to assess the damage. A foul, noxious odor drove them back. From the lead locomotive, they radioed headquarters to say, "We're getting the hell out of here!" They uncoupled the engine and ran it to Mt. Shasta, the next town up the line.

Despite the crew's report of noxious fumes, the first emergency responders on the scene weren't alerted to the possibly hazardous nature of the tanker car's contents or that a spill might have reached the river. This confusion continued into the following day. Southern Pacific representatives said the tanker car was punctured as it fell into the river. Others maintained that the leak was caused when Southern Pacific employees later tried to pull the car out of the water. They believed that the leak began a few hours after the derailment. Administrators with the California Department of Fish and Game said they had people at the scene within hours of the derailment, and they didn't detect a spill. They left the scene in charge of Southern Pacific officials and didn't learn anything about the leakage until the next day. The president of Southern Pacific later denied that members of his crew had touched the tanker car until it was pulled from the water three days later.

Regardless, someone finally double-checked the train's cargo manifest and discovered that the tanker car in the river was filled with "weed killer," which proved to be 19,000 gallons of metam sodium. They immediately notified local railroad supervisors, the California Office of Emergency

Services, California Department of Fish and Game, and Siskiyou County Sheriff's Office. As emergency responders soon discovered, the tanker car had suffered three punctures. When the metam sodium inside hit the water, it broke down into the gas hydrogen sulfide and the chemical methyl isothiocyanate, which also gives off a toxic gas.

Soon, a toxic plume of pea-green foam was floating down the river, and noxious gases that smelled of rotten eggs drifted into Dunsmuir, making it difficult for residents to breathe. People crowded into doctors'

Railcars rest in the Upper Sacramento River
near Dunsmuir at Cantara Loop.
PHOTOGRAPH COURTESY OF THE CALIFORNIA
DEPARTMENT OF FISH AND WILDLIFE.

offices and local hospitals complaining of headaches, dizziness, nausea, and skin and eye irritation. Local city and county officials evacuated some people from homes along the river, but the evacuation was voluntary. They also posted signs warning people not to fish in the river. State park rangers went to every local campground to evacuate all campers, and a sixty-mile stretch of Interstate 5 was closed. Emergency shelters were set up in two of the high schools, and more than 100 people came seeking help.

Warnings about the dangers caused by the spill were inconsistent. Some people were told to leave windows open to ventilate their houses. Others were told to keep windows closed to keep the toxic fumes out. Construction workers at nearby sites were told that coming to work the next day was "voluntary." Some were asked to sign waivers saying that they'd been warned of the dangers. A few local companies advised their workers to limit their exposure time to four hours. Yet scientists were not allowed near the water for the next three days.

As the chemical soup made its way downriver, it killed all aquatic life in its path. An estimated 1 million fish were killed, including 300,000 trout and 650,000 riffle sculpin. In an ABC News report looking back on the disaster twenty years later, a state Fish and Game biologist reported, "We were loading up . . . garbage bags full of dead fish. It wasn't just dead fish though, it was crayfish, it was sculpin, it was hordes of invertebrates, aquatic insects, and salamanders." In short, the spill wiped out the foundation of the river's food chain. As lethal to plants as it was to animals, the metam sodium also killed up to 80 percent of the alders and 40 percent of the cottonwood trees lining the riverbanks.

The poison gradually coursed downstream and arrived at Shasta Lake, California's largest reservoir, on Wednesday, July 17. Not a single organism—not one fish, amphibian, or aquatic insect—was left alive along that thirty-eight-mile stretch of the Sacramento River. Stan Statham, an assemblyman who represented the area in the state legislature, viewed the site from the air. He said it was "one of the worst ecological river spills ever on record in our north state." Dead fish floated everywhere and were lodged beneath rocks. Some people began calling it the Dead River.

If there was any good news, it was that officials were able to stop releasing water from Shasta Lake and contain the toxic plume. The reservoir was the main water supply for the Central Valley Project, which provided water to farms and about 10 million California households. Luckily, instead of spreading throughout the lake, the poison remained relatively concentrated in a blob 18 feet thick, 100 yards wide, and three-quarters of a mile long. It collected 18 to 36 feet below the surface.

Chemical-spill specialists with Southern Pacific devised an elaborate plan to disperse the toxin: they positioned a ring of barges around the poisonous blob and pumped air into the lake beneath it. Pumps on the barges also sucked up tainted water and sprayed it into the air. Both techniques helped to dilute and dissipate the chemicals. The plan worked well enough to prevent massive fish kills in the lake. Soon, contamination levels in the river and lake were below the thresholds set by state health regulations.

The 1991 metam sodium spill killed 1 million fish in the Upper Sacramento River.
PHOTOGRAPH COURTESY OF THE CALIFORNIA DEPARTMENT OF FISH AND WILDLIFE.

Scientists assured the public that any wildlife that fed on the dead fish—such as eagles, bears, raccoons, and river otters—wouldn't be sickened or killed by toxins in the fish. While this turned out to be true, animals that relied on fish and other aquatic prey soon found that their food source was gone.

Investigators determined that the cause of the accident was a faulty locomotive incapable of pulling its load of cars uphill, as well as improper sequencing of loaded and empty cars. As the locomotive crossed the Cantara Loop bridge, one or more wheels slipped. When the wheels regained traction, the forward surge of power created too much sidewise force on the cars at the hairpin curve, flipping them off the tracks.

Not long after the accident, the people of Dunsmuir called for an investigation into Southern Pacific operations. Townspeople knew that the rail line through the canyon was prone to trouble; in the previous sixteen years, there had been twenty-one train accidents on or near the Cantara Loop.

Prior to this accident, the U.S. Environmental Protection Agency (EPA) had not included metam sodium on its list of hazardous materials requiring special handling during shipment. After the accident, the EPA prohibited the use of metam sodium in homes and gardens. Farmers using the chemical were warned to wear respirators, long-sleeve shirts, and chemical-resistant gloves and boots.

The U.S. Fish and Wildlife Service, California Department of Fish and Game, and other agencies conducted a Natural Resource Damage Assessment to determine which parties were responsible for the damage to fish and wildlife and what they should pay for it. The funds went into a grant program that was overseen by the Cantara Trustee Council. These funds were used for resource acquisition, protection, recovery, and monitoring.

The railroad assumed much of the responsibility for the disaster and took several steps to atone for the damage and prevent similar problems in the future. Recognizing the danger posed by the Cantara Loop, Southern Pacific built a high-strength barrier along the curve to prevent cars from reaching the river in the event of future derailments. The railroad agreed to pay more than $30 million to the federal government and the State of California as reimbursement for costs incurred as a result of the spill, including legal fees and ongoing monitoring costs. It was the largest settlement of its kind in California history. The company that owned the punctured railcar and the company that leased it paid another $6 million to federal agencies. The company that produced the weed killer also agreed to pay $2 million and to begin labeling tanker cars that carried metam sodium.

Residents of Dunsmuir filed 1,735 claims against Southern Pacific. Some of these were for property damage and some were based on an expected loss of future income due to a collapsed fishing and tourist trade. Many claims were health-related. About 500 Dunsmuir residents had sought medical attention for headaches, nosebleeds, and rashes and other skin ailments. Several babies were born prematurely. At a town meeting held in August, people were still angry. Many wanted to recall the mayor and councilmen for the way the spill had been handled. In a separate settlement, the railroad paid $13.5 million to satisfy citizen claims.

As the years passed, this stretch of river recovered more quickly than many thought possible. Just ten years after the spill, Craig Martz, a planning director for the California Department of Fish and Game, commented on the recovery of life in the river. He said fish were teeming again, and they appeared to be a little larger on average than before the toxic spill. A snorkel survey suggested that there were about 2,000 fish per river mile and that these averaged ten to twelve inches long. Aquatic insect populations also rebounded well. With good hatches of stoneflies, caddisflies, and mayflies, not only was there food for fish but also for the frogs, salamanders, and songbirds that returned to the area.

A few types of organisms haven't recovered, including some species of snails, clams, and crayfish. Bottom-dwelling fish called sculpin, which before the spill were the most abundant fish in the river, have been slow to return. Trees have also been slow to recolonize along some parts of the river. After the spill, the California Fish and Game stopped planting large numbers of hatchery trout in this part of the river.

A few years after the spill, Southern Pacific was purchased by Union Pacific Railroad. Ten years after the accident, Union Pacific placed a plaque at the Cantara Loop to commemorate the work of volunteers from the region who contributed to the restoration and maintenance of the river's ecology.

Astonishingly, in 2003 another derailment near the Cantara Loop came close to re-creating the 1991 disaster. Five cars in a Union Pacific train ended up in the river, some of them holding residue of ammonium-nitrate fertilizer. If those cars had been full and ruptured, the chemical would've killed thousands of fish. Another car that derailed was full of hydrochloric acid, which also would've killed fish if it had reached the river.

SANTA FE–UNION PACIFIC COLLISION, 1994

The 1989 Southern Pacific train wreck described at the beginning of this chapter was not the last to occur on the infamous Cajon Pass. Only five years after the Duffy Street incident, on December 14, 1994, a runaway freight train crashed into the rear end of another freight train stopped on the tracks just below the pass.

A fifty-four-car freight train operated by the Atchison, Topeka, and Santa Fe Railway was carrying furniture from Birmingham, Alabama, to Los Angeles. Before beginning the descent of Cajon Pass, crew members had stopped to test the brakes, which checked out okay.

Near the junction of California Highway 138 and Interstate 15, an eighty-two-car Union Pacific freight train had paused on its journey from Provo, Utah, to Los Angeles, carrying coal destined for Japan. The Union Pacific train had stopped for a red signal that indicated another train ahead needed to switch tracks. The crew was monitoring the radio when they suddenly heard frantic calls to the dispatcher—the Santa Fe crew had lost control of their train. The normal speed for that six-mile stretch of track with a 3 percent downhill grade is fifteen miles per hour, but the Santa Fe train had lost its brakes and was traveling at about forty-five miles per hour.

The Union Pacific crew ran from their train. One later said, "We saw the headlights and we bailed." The Santa Fe crew had the same idea, jumping off just seconds before the collision. The impact derailed five locomotives and five cars. A fire broke out and burned for hours, with flames easily visible to passing motorists on Interstate 15.

The two Santa Fe crewmen were injured in their leap from the rolling train; one suffered blunt abdominal trauma and the other a chest injury and spinal fracture. Both eventually recovered. Although no lives were lost, the collision destroyed four Santa Fe locomotives and two Union Pacific locomotives, along with numerous freight cars. Monetary losses were estimated at over $4 million.

CHATSWORTH TRAIN COLLISION, 2008

Of course, train accidents have happened elsewhere in California, too. And sometimes the cause is one that's increasingly familiar to motorists in our always-connected, social-media-driven society.

On the afternoon of Friday, September 12, 2008, Metrolink passenger train engineer Robert Sanchez, forty-six, pulled out of the Chatsworth station northwest of Los Angeles with 222 people on board. Sanchez was in control of Train 111, a locomotive pulling three two-level coaches. A little over a mile west of the station, at 4:22 P.M., Train 111 rounded a curve and ran head-on into an eastbound Union Pacific freight train. The Union Pacific train included two locomotives pulling seventeen freight cars. Both trains were traveling at about forty-two miles per hour. The freight train

The Metrolink locomotive crushed much of the lead passenger car.
PHOTOGRAPH COURTESY OF CRAIG WIGGENHORN, CC BY-SA 3.0.

engineer applied the brakes two seconds before the collision; Sanchez, in the Metrolink locomotive, never hit the brakes.

The Metrolink locomotive and lead passenger car derailed. The locomotive telescoped fifty-two feet into the lead passenger car, killing twenty-five people including Sanchez. The two locomotives and ten cars of the Union Pacific train derailed. The freight train's conductor and engineer were trapped in the lead locomotive and surrounded by flames until rescuers pulled them free. A brakeman in the second locomotive was also injured, but all three Union Pacific crew members survived.

Local hospitals struggled to cope with the arrival of injured passengers. At least 135 people were injured, 46 of them critically. All twelve trauma centers in Los Angeles County received patients.

Total damages were estimated to be $12 million. Investigators with the National Transportation Safety Board determined that the primary cause of the wreck was that Sanchez had been distracted while texting on his cell phone and missed a red signal light warning of the oncoming Union Pacific train. Supervisors had already warned Sanchez twice about improper use of cell phones while on duty. The California Public Utilities Commission quickly issued an emergency order banning the use of cell phones by train crews, and one week after the accident a law was passed that banned texting while driving an automobile in California.

SOURCES

San Bernardino Train Wreck

Beitler, Stu. "San Bernardino, CA Train Derailment Kills Several, May 1989." GenDisasters.com.

Martin, Hugo. "'89 Rail, Pipe Disaster Has a Bitter Echo." *Los Angeles Times*. February 16, 2004.

Railroad Accident Report. Derailment of Southern Pacific Transportation Company Freight Train on May 12, 1989 and Subsequent Rupture of CalNev Petroleum Pipeline on May 25, 1989. National Transportation Safety Board. PB90-916302 NTSB/RAR-90/02.

Dunsmuir Train Derailment and Toxic Spill

Bunting, Glenn F. and Janine DeFao. "EPA Admits Failure on Chemical in Toxic Spill." *Los Angeles Times*. October 4, 1991.

Clarke, Chris. "This Widely Used Pesticide Caused California's Worst Inland Environmental Disaster." Kcet.org. April 6, 2017.

DuPertuis, Richard. "Dunsmuir reaped benefits from 1991 disaster." Mtshastanews.com. July 27, 2011.

Final Report on the Recovery of the Upper Sacramento River Subsequent to the 1991 Cantara Spill. Cantara Trustee Council. 2007.

Gehrman, Ed. "A Toxic Nightmare: The Dunsmuir Metam Sodium Spill Revisited." *Sonoma County Free Press*. July 1997.

Hazardous Substances & Public Health. Agency for Toxic Substances and Disease Registry, Public Health Service, U.S. Department of Health and Human Services. Volume 3, Number 4. January 1994.

Johns, Brian. "Southern Pacific Settles 1991 Chemical Spill Suit." JOC.com. March 15, 1994.

Jones, Ray and Joe Lubow. *Disasters and Heroic Rescues of California.* Guilford, CT: The Globe Pequot Press, 2006.

Martin, Glen. "Dunsmuir, 10 years later/upper Sacramento River alive after deadly pesticide spill." SFGate. July 9, 2001.

Natural Resource Damage and Restoration Program. Southern Pacific Railroad Metam Sodium Spill. U.S. Department of the Interior. No date.

Paddock, Richard. "Firms to Pay $40 Million in '91 River Spill." *Los Angeles Times.* March 15, 1994.

Train Derailments and Toxic Spills: Hearing Before the Government Activities and Transportation Sub-Committee of the Committee on Government Operations, House of Representatives, One Hundred Second Congress, First Session, October 3, 1991. U.S. Government Printing Office, Washington, D.C., 1992.

Warren, Jenifer. "Sacramento River Hit by Pesticide Spill." *Los Angeles Times.* July 16, 1991.

Santa Fe–Union Pacific Collision

Associated Press. "A Runway Train Slams a Halted One." *The New York Times.* December 15, 1994.

Gorman, Tom. "Runaway Train Hits Another in Cajon Pass." *Los Angeles Times.* December 15, 1994.

Wald, Matthew L. "Inspectors Failed to See Brake Problem on Train that Derailed." *The New York Times.* March 7, 1996.

Chatsworth Train Collision

Railroad Accident Report. Collision of Metrolink Train 111 with Union Pacific Train LOF65-12, Chatsworth, California, September 12, 2008. National Transportation Safety Board. January 21, 2010. PB2010-916301.

Solomon, Brian. *North American Locomotives: A Railroad-by-Railroad Photohistory.* New York, NY: Crestline, 2017.

DROUGHT AND DUST STORMS

RELENTLESS DROUGHT, 2011–2017

CALIFORNIA'S CLIMATE HAS LONG ALTERNATED BETWEEN WET AND dry periods. Significant droughts that last a few years at a time strike six times a century on average. Tree-ring studies reveal that this cycle goes back to at least the twelfth century. In modern times, a crippling two-year drought hit California in the mid-1970s, but a drought from 2011 through 2017 was particularly severe and prolonged. It produced a slow-rolling disaster in its own right, as this chapter describes, but it also primed the state for devastating wildfires and mudslides in subsequent years. (See Chapters 14 and 5, respectively.)

Kevin Anchukaitis, a geochronologist at Woods Hole Oceanographic Institution in Massachusetts, and his associates determined that the 2011–2017 drought in California was the region's worst in at least 1,200 years. He said, "Almost always when we look back in time it's been drier at some time. Not only did this . . . drought rank among the handful of driest years, it appears to have been the worst." This determination was made through scientific study of geological markers in the environment, such as sediments in lake beds, stalagmites in caves, and the rings of ancient trees.

According to the National Oceanic and Atmospheric Administration (NOAA), December 2011 was the second-driest December in California history, with many parts of the state experiencing record or near-record dry conditions. That month, Fresno received no measurable precipitation, and San Francisco saw only 0.14 inch of rain. Dry weather persisted, and by April 2012 half of California was in "severe" drought.

Drought conditions across the United States are categorized on a weekly map called the U.S. Drought Monitor, produced by the National Drought Mitigation Center at the University of Nebraska-Lincoln. The map shows five levels of dry conditions: abnormally dry (D0), moderate drought (D1), severe drought (D2), extreme drought (D3), and exceptional drought (D4). Damage to crops begins to occur at D1, and crop losses appear at D2, often leading resource managers to impose water-use restrictions.

Much of the Central Valley and Southern California baked under extreme high temperatures through the summer of 2012. That winter brought below-average amounts of rain and snow, especially in the regions where it was most needed. Then the sky quit delivering water—California received less rainfall in 2013 than in any year on record. Without rain to recharge them, reservoirs and soil moisture across the state were depleted. Streams and rivers dwindled to warm trickles or dried up completely, harming fish populations. The state fisheries chief estimated that 95 percent of the offspring from the winter chinook salmon run didn't survive. And still the rains didn't come. By mid-January 2014, more than half the state was categorized as D3 (extreme drought). On January 17, 2014, Governor Jerry Brown declared a state of emergency and asked towns and cities to voluntarily reduce water usage by 25 percent.

The governor's action was too little too late, and drought conditions continued. By spring of 2014, snowpack was near zero, and for the first time on record the entire state was categorized as D2 (severe drought) or worse. In fact, much of the state—from San Diego to the Oregon border—was in extreme drought (D3), and an apple-shaped region from the Bay Area to Santa Barbara and east to Fresno was in exceptional drought (D4).

By the beginning of 2015, more than half of California was in exceptional drought (D4). In March, the water content of the Sierra snowpack was only 5 percent of normal, so there was nothing to refill the reservoirs that watered the state's crops and suburban lawns. In 2015, the average annual temperature in California was higher than at any time in the previous 120 years. The year also turned out to be the second driest on record.

In the heart of the drought, Californians experienced a wide range of impacts and challenges. Water-use restrictions meant that lawns and crops withered, golf courses turned brown, swimming pools sat empty, and dust settled on everything. Children no longer spent the summer running through sprinklers or squirting one another with hoses. People took shorter showers and flushed toilets less often. Every drop of water was precious.

Consider the plight of Okieville, a hamlet about seven miles west of Tulare in the San Joaquin Valley between Fresno and Bakersfield. Officially named Highland Acres, locals called it Okieville after the people who migrated there in the 1930s to escape the Dust Bowl on the Great Plains.

Central Valley farmlands baked under the sun during the relentless drought in 2015.
PHOTOGRAPH BY KELLY GROW, COURTESY OF THE CALIFORNIA
DEPARTMENT OF WATER RESOURCES.

The unofficial mayor of Okieville, Marvin May, was one of those Dust Bowl migrants. He came to California when he was only seven years old. During his half century in Okieville, May had watched the hamlet grow from two homes to a hundred. The community boasted green lawns and gardens. Most of the residents worked on farms and dairies in Tulare County, one of the top-producing agricultural areas in the country. During the 2011–2017 drought, Okieville was one of the hardest hit communities in the state. Wells dried up and, by the summer of 2015, one-quarter of the homes in Okieville were without water.

In rural Tulare County, more than 1,700 wells went dry by the fall of 2015. Only the deepest wells continued to yield water. Many residents of Okieville carried buckets to a neighbor's house to get water from their well. Some neighbors ran a hose from their well to another's home. The state stepped in to deliver bottled water to Okieville residents, and some residents installed tanks that they could get filled by a state water truck. Finally, the residents used $2.6 million in emergency drought funding to drill a deep community well and install piping and metering for each home. While this deeper well seemed like a more permanent solution, it will provide water only if rains and snowmelt continue to recharge the aquifer beneath the valley. If climate change brings more frequent and prolonged droughts, even deep wells could go dry.

Household use accounts for about 20 percent of human water consumption. State and local officials encouraged and then mandated various conservation measures, restricting lawn watering, leaving swimming pools empty, and using water more efficiently when washing clothes and dishes, showering, and flushing toilets. These measures cut household water use between 2013 and early 2016 statewide by about 25 percent.

But agriculture is California's largest water consumer—the state produces about half of all the fruits, nuts, and vegetables grown in the United States. All of these thirsty crops depend on a complex system of water management overseen by federal, state, and local agencies. Some water has to be allowed to flow downstream to sustain fisheries and aquatic ecosystems. And at times, water must be stored to prevent flooding. More than fifty large reservoirs around the state store water for use in drier months. During this prolonged drought, nearly every reservoir dwindled to a small fraction of its normal capacity. Farmers responded by planting fewer crops; in 2014, almost 500,000 acres of normally productive farmland were left idle.

During times of normal precipitation in California, 40 percent of the water used each year comes from groundwater sources, but by 2014 that had increased to 60 percent. Because of the drought, farmers in 2015 received about 50 percent less surface water. To make up for this loss, they pumped additional groundwater. Even then, they still had about 10 percent less water than in a normal year. In places where access to groundwater was limited, the impact to crops and agricultural jobs was more severe. Also, pumping groundwater tends to cost more than diverting surface sources, and those costs were passed on as higher food prices.

Thousands of farm jobs were lost during the drought. As farmers reduced their crops, fewer field hands and other workers were needed. Tulare County saw a 19 percent drop in available jobs during the drought. Many of these people began to travel long distances to find work or, unemployed, relied on food stamps and other public assistance. One-fourth of the families in Tulare County were reduced to poverty level. Many moved away, and some rural schools recorded large drops in enrollment. Small businesses in rural towns were also affected. They had fewer customers with less money. Crime increased.

Drought affects many aspects of life, including public health. There was more dust in the air, and smoke from wildfires reduced air quality, sometimes to hazardous levels. During the drought, more people sought treatment for asthma, bronchitis, and allergies. There was also an eightyfold increase in human cases of West Nile virus, a potentially deadly disease transmitted by mosquitoes. When rural streams and ponds dried up, mosquitoes moved into urban areas in search of water. They thrive especially in stagnant water, which was more readily available. Plus, warmer temperatures lengthened the mosquito season. Cases of Valley Fever, a fungal respiratory disease, also increased as more spores were carried on the dust.

The drought dramatically affected the environment. Fish such as salmon and smelt struggled to migrate and spawn. Water levels in the Sacramento-San Joaquin Delta were so low that the Delta smelt, a once common species, became endangered. Courts ordered water-use restrictions to improve flows. In the Klamath River in Northern California, chinook salmon also became endangered and needed water for their annual run. In August 2015, the U.S. Bureau of Reclamation released extra water from Trinity Reservoir to save the fish. In some places, mouths of rivers were blocked by sandbars, so ocean fish couldn't reach their spawning rivers. Low flows also led to higher stream and lake temperatures, which can be harmful or deadly to many fish and aquatic organisms. Lake Tahoe warmed three degrees Fahrenheit each year from 2012 to 2015.

Animals and birds were also adversely affected by the years of drought. Honeybees suffered due to the lack of wildflowers. The average production of honey per colony dropped from 100 pounds to 40 pounds. Even large mammals like bears had a hard time. As they prepared for hibernation, they roamed widely, even into towns, seeking food.

Trees also suffered during the drought. Millions of them died in the Sierra Nevada, and foresters were concerned for the health of giant sequoias and coastal redwoods. Near the end of 2016, the U.S. Forest Service announced that 102 million trees had died in California since 2010 and that 62 million of these had died in 2016 alone. Dying trees and dry vegetation in the spring and fall made for a large number of forest fires and set the stage for the massively destructive fire seasons of 2017 and 2018 (see Chapter 14).

Many of California's reservoirs generate hydroelectric power. As water levels in the reservoirs dropped to historic lows, the ability to generate power also declined—by 36 percent over the course of the drought. To compensate, more people turned to natural gas to produce electricity, and from 2012 to 2015 this released an extra 23 million tons of carbon dioxide into the atmosphere. The total additional cost to customers of generating extra power from natural gas during this period was about $2 billion.

Near the end of 2015, drought conditions in California began to improve, and in 2016 precipitation was average in Northern California, where most of the state's water supply originates. Finally, in April 2017, Governor Jerry Brown declared that the California drought was over, although problems resulting from the depletion of groundwater supplies remained. In 2018, California had a wet November and December, followed in 2019 by a very wet January, February, and March. The snowpack in the Sierras soared to 150 percent of normal. Conditions improved elsewhere, too. Less than halfway into the year, Los Angeles had already received more than its annual normal rainfall. In March 2019, the U.S. Drought Monitor map showed California as drought-free.

A number of factors likely combined to cause this particularly persistent drought. A high-pressure ridge formed off the West Coast for three winters in a row, diverting storms that ordinarily would have brought rains to the state. This high-pressure area was bolstered by La Niña and sea-surface temperatures. The NOAA Drought Task Force attributed the drought to natural variability in atmospheric and ocean conditions, but

In May 2021, Gov. Newsom hyped a $5.1 billion drought plan at the near-dry San Luis Reservoir.
PHOTOGRAPH BY ANDREW INNERARITY,
COURTESY OF THE CALIFORNIA DEPARTMENT OF WATER RESOURCES.

Stanford University researchers assert that global climate change was a critical factor.

SAN JOAQUIN VALLEY DUST STORMS

The broad San Joaquin Valley is known for being tops in the country for two things. First, it's one of the most productive agricultural areas in the United States. Second, the valley is hemmed in by mountains to the west, south, and east, so it suffers long periods of stagnant air, creating some of the worst air pollution in the country. On occasion, mighty winds spill into the valley and wreak havoc. Such was the case when gales generated two of California's most destructive dust storms, first in the southern valley around Bakersfield in 1977 and again between Fresno and Coalinga in 1991.

THE GREAT BAKERSFIELD DUST STORM OF 1977

Forty years after the Bakersfield Dust Storm of 1977, journalist Harold Pierce, writing for the *Bakersfield Californian*, interviewed people who had lived through the incident. Several of them said they thought it was the end of the world. The wind howled and the dust was so thick it blotted out the sun. Aaron Reynolds, who was thirteen at the time, recalled that he decided to go out in style. He took his sleeping bag onto the roof of his house, made a sort of parachute, and waited for the dusty wind to take him away. He thought he would fly like the Wicked Witch in *The Wizard of Oz*. And fly he did—a gust lifted him right off the roof and tossed him smack into the backyard fence, breaking his wrist. It turned out not to be the end of the world, but it was a monster of a dust storm.

In December 1977, Southern California was at the end of a severe two-year drought. Soil moisture was at its lowest level in nearly half a

Dr. Joseph Poland stands next to signs on a telephone pole marking
how much the land has subsided due to groundwater withdrawals.
PHOTOGRAPH BY RICHARD IRELAND, COURTESY OF THE U.S. GEOLOGICAL SURVEY.

century, and growers in the San Joaquin Valley had pumped so much water out of the ground to irrigate crops that the surface had subsided by more than a foot in some places. By mid-December, fields had been plowed and planted, but the new crops hadn't yet had time to develop deep roots. Thousands of acres of bare soil faced the sky. Windbreaks in the valley were few and far between.

Around December 19, a strong high-pressure ridge moved south into the Great Basin region east of the Sierras. At the same time, an intense low-pressure system neared the coast of Northern California. The juxtaposition of these two systems produced a steep pressure gradient in the San Joaquin and Sacramento Valleys. That gradient meant that cool, dry desert air was drawn down the canyons of the Tehachapi Mountains southeast of Bakersfield. As it sank toward the valley, the air mass became compressed and heated, decreasing its relative humidity. The desert air became even drier.

Just before midnight on December 19, in communities throughout the southern San Joaquin Valley, the temperature began to rise and a light northwesterly wind shifted and began coming out of the southeast. It grew stronger through the night. By morning the wind was blowing squalls of dust. Scattered power outages hit Bakersfield, but people went to work and school as usual.

But by 9 A.M. on December 20, it had become obvious that this was an unusually strong storm. School was canceled. Parents were asked to pick up their children out of concern that high-profile buses might be blown over by the increasingly strong winds.

By late morning, roads in Kern County leading into the southern end of the San Joaquin Valley were closed. Airborne dust blotted out the sun. Power outages were widespread, interrupting the broadcasts of storm bulletins, and only a few small AM radio stations were available to broadcast information locally. Billboards and business signs began blowing down. Windows in homes shattered and roofs peeled away. At the Three-Way

Research indicates that dust storms will become more frequent
as climate change leads to longer droughts.
PHOTOGRAPH COURTESY OF THE NATIONAL OCEANIC AND ATMOSPHERIC ADMINISTRATION.

Chevrolet auto showroom in Bakersfield, the plate glass windows blew
out and scattered glass over the new cars. The wind sandblasted paint off
the cars and pitted their chrome bumpers. Dust seeped inside buildings
through cracks. The gymnasium floor in one closed school was covered in a
quarter inch of dust.

In the small town of Arvin between Bakersfield and the Tehachapi
Mountains, an anemometer broke when the winds hit 88 miles per hour.
The U.S. Geological Survey later estimated that gusts as high as 192 miles
per hour roared through town, and nearby mountain passes saw 199-mile-
per-hour winds. Arvin resident LeRoy Schnell said that gravel the size of
peas was blowing in the wind. The air was so filled with dirt that it was as
dark as night at midday.

John Kovacevich was at work in Arvin when his office windows exploded inward. He took that as a sign to stop for the day and go home, but
visibility was so poor as he drove that he followed a pair of taillights right
off the road and 100 yards into a plowed field, wondering why the road

was so bumpy. Kovacevich was able to get back onto the road and ended up staying with friends nearby until conditions improved. He was lucky: thousands of motorists on Interstate 5 and California Highway 58 were trapped in their cars for hours.

As the winds hit the valley, they lifted exposed soil and carried it aloft. The plume of dust looked like a tidal wave rising more than 5,000 feet above the valley floor. Twenty-five million metric tons of soil were stripped off grazing and farm land in just twenty-four hours. In places, livestock were buried alive, whole almond orchards were knocked down, and canals were filled with dirt. Roads became covered in sand. One driver stopped his car because he could no longer see where to drive. The front window of his car blew out and the driver left the car seeking shelter. He was found three days later, lucky to be alive but suffering from hypothermia and skin burns from the blowing dirt.

In Fresno, it began to rain. When the dust mixed with the rain, sheets of mud fell from the sky. The dust from this storm dimmed the sun as far away as Reno, Nevada, and was later found as an embedded layer in the snow on Mount Shasta, 500 miles to the north.

Some of the damage from this dust storm wasn't apparent immediately. The wind-stripped land in the Tehachapi Mountains contributed to run-off and flooding when the next rains came. In the year after the storm, the Kern County Public Health Services Department counted 451 cases of Valley Fever, a 61 percent increase over the previous year. Seven people died from this fungal respiratory infection. One eleven-year-old girl survived being lifted by the wind and dropped into her family's mud-filled swimming pool only to later fall ill with Valley Fever. Her father got sick, too, but both recovered.

In all, the storm killed five people (not including the Valley Fever victims) and caused more than $34 million in damages. The National Weather Service ranked it as one of the top fifteen weather events of the century.

1991 DUST STORM

Another dust storm struck the lower San Joaquin Valley on November 29, 1991, the Friday after Thanksgiving. Again, a prolonged drought—this one lasting five years—preceded the wind event. Almost no rain had fallen for the previous nine months, and the farmland along Interstate 5 was dry and bare. Because of the lack of rain, many farmers had decided not to plant.

Motorists driving home after the holiday created heavy traffic on Interstate 5. Then, about 2:30 P.M. twenty miles north of Coalinga, a dust storm developed in a matter of minutes. As winds jumped to forty and then sixty miles per hour, dust blew across the highway, greatly reducing visibility. Apparently many motorists ignored the deteriorating conditions and continued driving at high speeds. When one car finally slowed, it was struck from behind, and this set off a chain-reaction collision that eventually involved 104 vehicles, including eleven semi-trailers. (It's possible even more vehicles were involved, but some people with minor damage simply exchanged information and drove away.)

Unable to see, motorists kept slamming into the wrecked cars ahead. Some people climbed out of their cars, dazed and bleeding, and were immediately covered in blowing dust. Soon there were four pileups in the southbound lane and one in the northbound lane, each involving up to thirty vehicles. The wreckage was scattered along 1.5 miles of highway. Some vehicles caught fire.

One driver slammed into the rear wheel of a tractor trailer, and within seconds three other cars slammed into him, crushing his car like an accordion. The driver and his wife took the only escape route possible—they climbed out a window and pulled their children, who were in the back seat, out with them. One child was unconscious. Although they were injured, this whole family survived. Another motorist said he was stopped with no way ahead. When he saw a huge semi-trailer bearing down on him, he thought he would be killed. Instead, the truck driver veered off the road, tipping over his rig but avoiding a collision with the car.

The dust storm made medical assistance and rescue efforts extremely difficult. Even though the accident took place twenty miles from the nearest town, the first rescuers arrived within half an hour. Some victims were treated by a doctor and two Northern California firefighters who happened to be involved in the pileup. Every emergency vehicle from Coalinga and Los Banos, as well as those from Merced and Hanford, were summoned. An ambulance on the way to the scene collided with another vehicle. A fire truck was rear-ended, jamming the truck's back door and blocking access to the "Jaws of Life" tool needed to pry victims from crushed vehicles.

A truck driver hauling vegetables from San Francisco to Los Angeles managed to safely steer his 18-wheeler off the road. He began to carry victims both living and dead from their cars to the side of the road, where eventually they were lined up on stretchers. It took four hours to provide aid to all the injured. Officials set up a triage area about one mile east of the interstate in a vegetated area with far less blowing dust. Helicopters carried the most seriously injured people to ten hospitals in Fresno. Those with less serious injuries were taken to hospitals in Coalinga and Fresno by bus.

Jerry Scharton, who served with the U.S. Air Force Reserve and worked for the Mid-Land Fire Department, told a *New York Times* reporter: "It reminded me of the desert operation we had just had over there in the Gulf. There were cars that caught fire and some that were off the road upside down. Some were five abreast that looked like they had run into a brick wall. Trucks were jackknifed on both sides of the road."

Some motorists made their way to a nearby motel diner and exchanged stories about their ordeal. Drivers described visibility as being zero at times as clouds of dust blasted across the highway.

California Highway Patrol officers spent the night trying to determine the sequence of events. They marked wrecked vehicles and diagrammed their locations. They said it would take months to fully analyze the data.

Speed was clearly a key factor in the accidents, but the storm had come up so quickly that motorists had little time to adjust. Even those who weren't speeding or who had pulled over to stop still became entangled in the pileup because visibility was so poor.

A 150-mile section of Interstate 5 was closed for twenty-seven hours. Wreckers began moving in at dawn on Saturday to remove the damaged cars. Thousands of people in backed-up traffic were trapped in their vehicles all day. These were the lucky ones: they lost some time but not their lives. Many of the cars and trucks hauled away by work crews the day after the storm were so mangled and burned that they were almost unrecognizable.

Mindful of the need to reopen the interstate to accommodate the holiday traffic, crews worked quickly. At one point, they stopped when they learned that one truck in the pileup carried potentially explosive, industrial-sized oxygen tanks. Luckily, the tanks proved to be empty. Interstate 5 reopened about 7 P.M. on Saturday. Crews had quickly patched several areas where the pavement was gouged, and signs were posted warning motorists of the rough road.

Seventeen people were killed in the pileups and 150 were seriously injured. Two bodies were burned so badly that they couldn't be identified. This wasn't the worst traffic accident in California's history. There have been more fatalities in bus crashes and some huge pileups in ground-fog conditions, but this was the deadliest crash in California history involving a dust storm.

SOURCES

Relentless Drought, 2011–2017

"California Drought 2011–2017." *Climate Signals*. December 4, 2018.

"California is no stranger to dry conditions, but the drought from 2011–2017 was exceptional." Story map. National Integrated Drought Information System, U.S. Drought Portal.

Craig, Sarah. "How Drought-Hit Okieville, California, Is Coping with Dry Wells." *News Deeply*, The New Humanitarian. November 1, 2016.

Howitt, Richard et al. *Economic Analysis of the 2015 Drought for California Agriculture*. University of California-Davis Center for Watershed Sciences, ERA Economics, UC Agricultural Issues Center. 2015.

Kobasa, Paul A., editor in chief. *Droughts*. World Book, Inc., 2018.

Perdew, Laura. *The California Drought*. Abdo Publishing, 2018.

Stevens, Matt. "Water, 2015, California: The no-good, very bad year. Now—pray for rain." *Los Angeles Times*. September 29, 2015.

Sumner, Thomas. "California drought worst in at least 1,200 years." *Science News*. December 6, 2014.

San Joaquin Valley Dust Storms

Chandler, John. "14 Killed, 114 Hurt in I-5 Pileups." *Los Angeles Times*. November 30, 1991.

Chandler, John and Mark Stein. "I-5 Is Reopened after Pileup that Killed 15." *Los Angeles Times*. December 1, 1991.

Drought, Heat Waves, and Dust Storms. San Francisco, CA: The Great Courses, 2016.

Pollack, Andrew. "Scenes of Disaster in Pileup that Killed 17 in California." *The New York Times*. December 1, 1991.

United Press International. "Deadly I-5 dust storm hit 'without warning.'" UPI.com. December 1, 1991.

Wilshire, H. G., J. K. Nakata, and Bernard Hallet. "Field observations of the December 1977 wind storm, San Joaquin Valley, California." *Desert Dust: Origin, Characteristics, and Effects on Man*. Geological Society of America, 1981.

WILDFIRES

WILDFIRES ARE A NATURAL FORCE THAT SHAPES THE CALIFORNIA landscape, but they've become more cataclysmic in modern times, growing larger, more destructive, and more costly. This is due in part to a warming and more volatile climate that primes conditions for major fires. It's also due to ever-increasing development, with the human footprint of homes, businesses, and infrastructure expanding into forests and across chaparral and grasslands. Here are stories from the worst of the most recent wildfires, including the largest to date in the history of modern-day California.

THE WILDFIRES OF 2017

According to the California Department of Forestry and Fire Prevention (CAL FIRE), 2017 saw the worst wildfire season the state had experienced up to that time. A total of 9,133 fires burned more than 1,381,405 acres, destroyed 9,470 homes and other structures, and damaged another 810. They killed forty-seven people, including two firefighters. Estimated insured losses totaled more than $13 billion. And the 2017 fires weren't confined to the northern part of the state. Southern California also suffered heavy losses, especially with the Thomas Fire, which started in Ventura County.

In the spring of 2017, heavy rains fell on much of the state—a welcome respite from a prolonged drought. But by late fall, the height of California's fire season, lush vegetation had dried out and set the stage for a series of especially destructive fires. The night of October 8 brought humidity of only about 12 percent, accompanied by strong winds. Wildfires ignited across Northern California. One cluster, which became known as the Northern California Fire Storm, began with the Tubbs Fire on the northern outskirts of Calistoga, in Napa County. Within three hours, thirty-mile-per-hour winds drove the fire twelve miles to the southwest into Sonoma County. In the inferno's path was the Safari West Wildlife Preserve, home to more than 1,000 exotic animals. Peter Lang, the seventy-two-year-old owner, fought the flames for ten hours using nothing more than garden hoses. Not a single animal perished in the fire.

But the winds grew stronger, and the fire soon approached Santa Rosa, the county seat. By 1 A.M. on October 9, the fire had entered city limits. Tens of thousands of people were evacuated with little notice. Firefighters made valiant efforts but could do little to stop the flames, which were driven by sixty-mile-per-hour winds. In the Coffey Park neighborhood, more than 1,300 homes burned to the ground. The fire reached U.S. Highway

The Tubbs Fire scorched more than 1,300 homes
in the Coffey Park neighborhood in Santa Rosa.
PHOTOGRAPH COURTESY OF THE CALIFORNIA HIGHWAY PATROL.

101 and destroyed the luxurious Fountaingrove Inn and a 250-room Hilton Hotel, along with a K-Mart store and several restaurants. By noon, 130 patients were being evacuated from the local Kaiser Permanente medical center, and Sutter Health was also evacuated. Also destroyed that day were the Redwood Adventist Academy, a senior-living complex, a primary school, and part of a winery. A high school and part of a performing-arts center both suffered damage.

By the morning of Thursday, October 12, the Tubbs Fire was only 10 percent contained. More than 20,000 acres had burned in Parkland and Bennett. Among the homes destroyed was that of the famed *Peanuts* cartoonist, Charles Schulz, whose widow, Jean Schulz, escaped unhurt.

Some residents of Northern California were reluctant to leave their homes when fire threatened and evacuation notices were given. One Napa County woman, Elaine Nicoletta, ignored the evacuation request three times before she finally agreed to leave, taking with her only the bare essentials. While speaking to KPIX CBS Bay Area News on October 13, she said she'd made peace with the fact that she might not see her home again: "Sure. It doesn't matter. The most important thing is your life and your family. And so, it is what it is. Once that fire comes through here, nothing can stop it."

Little was left in the aftermath of the fires in Santa Rosa.
PHOTOGRAPH COURTESY OF THE FEDERAL EMERGENCY MANAGEMENT AGENCY.

By October 31, when the Tubbs Fire was finally contained, it had burned 36,810 acres and killed twenty-two people in Sonoma County. It destroyed 2,900 homes in Santa Rosa. Economic losses to Santa Rosa alone totaled $1.2 billion, with another $100 million in fire suppression costs. Initially, blame fell on Pacific Gas & Electric Company equipment for starting the Tubbs Fire, but a sixteen-month investigation showed that it was started by a private electrical system next to a residential structure.

Other wine-country fires that sparked on October 8 included the Nuns Fire—which burned 56,556 acres, destroyed 1,355 structures, damaged another 172, and killed a couple in Glen Ellen—and the Atlas Fire north of the city of Napa, which burned 51,057 acres.

That same night, eighty miles to the north near Ukiah, the Potter Valley and Redwood Valley Fires merged and burned for twenty-one days, destroying 545 homes and other buildings and forcing the evacuation of 8,000 people. By the time the 36,523-acre fire was contained on October 28, twenty people had been hospitalized with severe burns and nine others, ranging in age from fourteen to eighty-eight, had died.

In December 2017, it was Southern California's turn to burn. On December 4, two fires ignited four miles and just thirty minutes apart when Southern California Edison electrical equipment sparked during sixty-mile-per-hour Santa Ana winds. The first fire started on a cattle ranch north of Santa Paula and just south of Thomas Aquinas College. The second blaze ignited in Upper Ojai at the top of Koenigstein Road. The fires soon merged, known as the Thomas Fire, and by late that night flames reached neighborhoods in the city of Ventura, burning 500 homes to the ground. The fire destroyed another 500 homes in small mountain communities nearby.

Surging winds with gusts over seventy miles per hour drove the fire west and north into Grant Park above Ventura City Hall, destroying homes and jumping California Highway 33 to burn through the Taylor Ranch oil fields all the way to U.S. Highway 101 and the Pacific Coast

The Thomas Fire kept firefighters busy for more than a month.
PHOTOGRAPH COURTESY OF THE SANTA BARBARA FIRE DEPARTMENT.

Highway. The governor called out the National Guard. The U.S. military brought in C-130 airplanes, and 290 fire engines came from Nevada, Arizona, Oregon, New Mexico, Utah, Idaho, and Montana. But fierce winds kept driving the inferno north and west across the Santa Ynez Mountains, threatening the Ojai Valley, Lake Casitas, and the communities of Carpenteria, Summerland, and Montecito. At times, the raging fire raced at a rate of an acre a second.

It wasn't until December 30 that the fire was more than 90 percent contained; fire officials decided to let any remaining flames within the perimeter die out on their own. On May 31, 2018, the Thomas Fire was officially declared out. By then, it had burned 281,893 acres, destroyed 1,063 structures, damaged at least 280 others, and claimed the life of an engineer working for the California Department of Forestry and Fire Prevention. Large portions of Ventura and Santa Barbara Counties were completely scorched. Damages totaled more than $2.2 billion, including suppression costs of $230 million. All told, more than 8,500 firefighters battled the Thomas Fire.

After an extremely dry year, rains finally arrived along the coast in early January 2018. But they fell on barren, burned-over slopes that were more ash than soil. Another type of disaster was in the making (see Chapter 5).

NO REST FOR THE WEARY—
2018 WILDFIRES

Californians endured a bad fire season in 2017. North and south, blazes caused death and destruction, and the Thomas Fire had been the largest in the state's modern history. Unfortunately, the new year brought little respite.

THE CARR FIRE

In the Redding area, the afternoon of July 23 was windy and hot—up to 100 degrees Fahrenheit. A travel trailer suffered a flat tire, and the metal rim sparked against the pavement near the intersection of California Highway 299 and Carr Powerhouse Road in the Whiskeytown-Shasta-Trinity Recreation Area west of Redding. The sparks ignited dry vegetation along the road, and winds fanned the flames. The blaze quickly grew to more than 20,000 acres and moved east toward Redding. Within days, the Carr Fire jumped the Sacramento River, and western neighborhoods in Redding were evacuated. Governor Jerry Brown declared a state of emergency.

The forest burns during the Carr Fire near Redding.
PHOTOGRAPH COURTESY OF CAL FIRE.

On July 26, a fire whirl developed in Redding, building into a rare phenomenon known as a fire tornado, with winds in excess of 143 miles per hour, equivalent to an EF3 tornado. This spinning vortex was on the ground from 7:30 to 8:00 P.M., knocking down transmission lines, shredding foliage, and stripping the bark from some trees while toppling others. Three people were killed in their home when the whirlwind blew out the walls and the roof collapsed on them. Other homes were also damaged by the tornado.

By the time the Carr Fire was fully contained on August 30, it had killed eight people, including three firefighters. It had burned 229,651 acres and destroyed 1,058 homes, causing $1.6 billion in damages.

THE MENDOCINO COMPLEX FIRES

While the Carr Fire was raging, two more fires started on July 27 near Ukiah. The Ranch and River Fires ignited within an hour of each other, forming what became known as the Mendocino Complex Fires. As in the Carr Fire, high temperatures, low humidity, and gusty winds fed the

An aircraft drops retardant on the Ranch Fire.
PHOTOGRAPH COURTESY OF CAL FIRE.

flames, expanding both fires. Red Flag conditions persisted, putting fire-fighters in danger as they struggled to save homes. Seven firefighters were injured in just the first few days of the fires. Then, on August 13, a falling tree hit Matthew Burchett, a forty-two-year-old battalion chief with the Draper, Utah, fire department. Burchett, who had volunteered to fight fire in California, later died of his injuries, leaving a wife and six-year-old son. On August 19, five more firefighters suffered burns; all eventually recovered.

Winds pushed the Ranch Fire northeast toward the Snow Mountain Wilderness in the North Coast Range of Mendocino National Forest. It continued to burn into January 2019 and was finally declared out 160 days after it began. It destroyed 280 structures and burned 410,203 acres, surpassing the previous year's record set by the Thomas Fire. Investigators later determined that the Ranch Fire started when a rancher trying to locate an underground wasp nest hammered a metal stake into the ground, creating a spark that lit dry grass.

While the Ranch Fire was smoldering, another fire took off in early November. Though less than half the size of the Ranch Fire, the Camp Fire grew to become the most deadly and destructive wildfire in the state's history. According to insurers, it was also the costliest natural disaster in the world in 2018.

THE CAMP FIRE

Hot, dry, gale-force winds from Nevada roared into California on the morning of November 8, 2018, funneling down Feather River Canyon in the Sierra Nevada. At 6:15 A.M., a Pacific Gas & Electric Company high-voltage line malfunctioned near the Poe Dam generating station about fourteen miles upstream from Lake Oroville, and a fire was reported at 6:29 A.M. Soon after, Captain Matt McKenzie of the California Division of Forestry and Fire Prevention at Jarbo Gap stood at the dam and watched the winds whip a ten-acre fire across the river. He had no way to reach it. The Camp Creek Road on the western side of the river was unpaved, steep, crumbling, and barely passable. Rockslides had almost erased parts of it. Recognizing the potential danger of this small fire, McKenzie radioed Pulga, a nearby community. An official evacuation order for Pulga came at 7:23 A.M. McKenzie requested fire engines, bulldozers, water tanks, and fire crews. He also requested helicopters and air tankers to fight the fire from above, but pilots couldn't take off because of the high winds.

Just five miles upslope from where the fire began, embers began raining down on the rural community of Concow. The roughly 700 residents tried to flee by car as trees and homes caught on fire around them. A fallen tree blocked the main escape route, Hoffman Road, so some people took refuge in a creek that fed Concow Reservoir. A fire captain and his crew deployed emergency shelters to try to protect people from the heat blast as the fire roared over them. When the fire passed, the firefighters radioed that they were coming out with three people who had burns over half their bodies. Eight people were dead.

Another small group from Concow jumped into Concow Reservoir to wait out the blaze in the frigid waters. Then they found rowboats and went to a tiny island. The fire surrounded the lake, but they were suffering from hypothermia. One man took a boat and went for help. He found Brandon Hill protecting his house with a garden hose. Hill's fourteen-year-old son, Daniel, grabbed an old canoe with some friends and rescued the shivering group from the island.

One man, fleeing the flames in his car, was blocked by a gate across the road. He left his car, jumped the gate, and followed a fox, also running for its life, into a small stream nearby. The flames burned over him as he huddled in the water, scorching his hair and clothes, but he survived. He made his way back to his car and found it and all the cars behind him destroyed by the fire.

As Concow burned, the fire chief of the old mining town of Paradise issued evacuation orders for the eastern quarter of town at 7:46 A.M. This community of 27,000 people had been threatened by a fire ten years earlier. At that time, evacuations had been ordered, and it had been evident that escape routes were inadequate. But instead of improving the roads, town leaders simply divided Paradise into fire zones and planned to evacuate one zone at a time. The Camp Fire would prove this decision to be a fatal mistake.

As the Camp Fire approached Paradise, the smoke, ash, and falling embers worsened. Schools had opened at 8 A.M. but closed thirty minutes later, creating chaos as parents came to pick up their children. At 8:30 A.M., falling embers set fire to a house in the middle of town. By 10 A.M., the roads were jammed, and traffic came almost to a standstill. Soon, fires were burning throughout town.

Not all parents were able to reach Ponderosa Elementary School to pick up their children; twenty-two children were stranded there. School bus driver Kevin McKay and two teachers loaded those pupils onto a bus, and McKay drove through the smoke until he was caught in the traffic gridlock. Many of the children on the bus were having trouble breathing in the heavy smoke, so McKay took off his shirt. He and the two teachers tore it into strips, soaked the strips in water from the one water bottle on board, and gave them to the children to hold over their faces to breathe through. This helped, and they continued moving slowly forward. Walls of flames flanked the bus on both sides of the road. McKay paused once to pick up a passenger, a preschool teacher whose car had broken down. It took five hours for the bus to reach safety and deliver the children to their grateful parents.

A building is lost to the flames during the Camp Fire in Paradise.
PHOTOGRAPH COURTESY OF CAL FIRE.

Smoke billows from the Camp Fire.
PHOTOGRAPH COURTESY OF CAL FIRE.

Tragically, most escape routes were clogged with vehicles as panicked people tried to escape. Power lines and several trees were down across Skyway Road, the main, four-lane road out of Paradise. Cars could only inch forward. Tires exploded from the heat of roadside flames, and aluminum rims melted onto the asphalt. Steering wheels went soft in the heat. As the fire intensified, people abandoned their cars and ran. In some cases, the soles of their shoes melted. The county dispatch system was quickly clogged with 911 calls from people trapped and needing assistance, including a woman in labor who was honking her car horn, trying to attract help.

The winds reached seventy-two miles per hour, whipping flames from one house to the next or leapfrogging embers far ahead of the fire front. Smoke filled the air. Faced with no escape, some people huddled in mowed fields, hoping the fire would pass over them. Others turned around and, miraculously, made it back to the hospital, which had been abandoned earlier. The main part of the hospital had not burned, and a clinic was set up in the emergency-room parking lot.

California Highway Patrolman Nick Powell had three evacuees in his SUV when another vehicle accidentally slammed into them, blowing his airbags. He waved down other vehicles to take his passengers, and then Powell ran from the fire until he was able to catch a ride on a fire truck.

Emergency responders were trying to reach Paradise, but hundreds of abandoned cars blocked their way. Fire crews tried to bump cars out of the way, and they called in bulldozers to help. Behind the bulldozers came buses to pick up and rescue people who had sought safety in fields. By 6 P.M. the fire had swept through Paradise, traveling 19 miles from its point of origin and covering more than 220 square miles. The list of people unaccounted for climbed to more than 300 names.

More than 5,400 firefighters attacked the fire, with support from aircraft. National Guard and search and rescue teams were dispatched to look for survivors. California Governor Jerry Brown visited the area but said he lacked words to describe the devastation.

On November 21, the Camp Fire reached the foothills east of Chico—people there had been wondering if and when it would reach them. Then their power went out. The Chico Fire Department issued an evacuation order on the evening of November 22 as flames spread toward U.S. Highway 99 and southeast Chico. But the weather finally cooperated, bringing much-needed precipitation. By November 25, steady rains helped to subdue the fire, and crews were able to declare it fully contained. But the 153,336-acre Camp Fire had killed eighty-six people and destroyed 18,733 structures, including 13,672 single-family homes. Damages were estimated at $16.5 billion. In February 2019, the Pacific Gas & Electric Company acknowledged that its equipment likely started the Camp Fire.

MASSIVE 2020 WILDFIRES

To date, the Camp Fire remains the deadliest wildfire in California history, but the 2020 fire season eclipsed all previous years in the sheer scope of devastation to the landscape. Five fires—all but one of which were sparked by lightning from dry thunderstorms in August—exceeded 300,000 acres in size, including the August Complex Fire, which torched an unprecedented 1,032,649 acres. Some of those fires continued to burn until mid-November.

A "perfect storm" of weather conditions aligned during the month of August 2020 to set the stage for this onslaught of wildfires. First, much of Northern and Central California experienced record-setting high temperatures from August 14 to 16, baking already dry vegetation. Then, beginning on August 16, remnants of Tropical Storm Fausto generated massive thunderstorms over much of the state. Unfortunately, the storms produced very little rain, while pounding the earth with lightning. The National Weather Service recorded more than 2,500 lightning strikes on the morning of the 16th in the Bay Area alone, at one point registering 200 strikes within thirty minutes. Over the next several days, more than 12,000 lightning strikes hit Northern California, starting an estimated 585 wildfires.

With so many fires burning simultaneously, CAL FIRE stopped naming them after local landmarks and instead used administrative codes. Brice Bennett, a CAL FIRE public information officer, explained, "We only group fires like that [into complexes] when we have a lightning siege as such." That's precisely what happened on August 16 and 17 across much of Northern and Central California.

THE NORTH COMPLEX FIRE

Lightning strikes on August 17 ignited twenty-one fires in the Plumas and Lassen National Forests about forty miles northeast of Chico. The largest of these were the Claremont and Bear Fires south of Quincy along the Middle Fork of the Feather River and near the Pacific Crest Trail. The fires merged on September 5, and over the next nine days strong winds drove the fire southwest, obliterating the town of Berry Creek, until it reached Lake Oroville and threatened the city of Oroville. The northern flank of

Firefighters work on the front line on the North Complex Fire.
PHOTOGRAPH COURTESY OF CAL FIRE.

the fire ran toward Concow, Paradise, and other communities that had burned in the 2018 Camp Fire. As of November 25, 2020, the North Complex Fire was 98 percent contained but had killed at least fifteen people, injured many more (including at least fifteen firefighters), destroyed more than 2,000 structures, and burned 318,935 acres.

THE SCU LIGHTNING COMPLEX FIRES

Lightning storms on August 16 started this cluster of distinct wildfires spanning six counties southeast of the Bay Area. Fires threatened the University of California's historic Lick Observatory on Mount Hamilton east of San Jose. Although flames destroyed and damaged nearby buildings, the observatory itself, which was completed in 1887, was spared. A total of 393,624 acres burned before the fires were contained on October 1, 2020.

THE LNU LIGHTNING COMPLEX FIRES

Lightning storms on August 17 sparked an astounding 250 fires across Northern California's wine country in Lake, Napa, Sonoma, Solano, and Yolo Counties. Though most of these fires were small, several of them merged into the 192,000-acre Hennessey Fire, which destroyed 1,491 homes and other buildings near the cities of Fairfield, Napa, and Vacaville. Thirty-mile-per-hour winds drove flames to the edge of downtown Vacaville, "right into people's backyards," according to one news report. Six people lost their lives in Sonoma and Solano Counties.

THE AUGUST COMPLEX FIRE

On the morning of August 17, thunderstorms rolled over Glenn and Mendocino Counties, dropping lightning and starting at least thirteen fires. One of these, the Doe Fire, thirty-five miles north of the small city of Willows, grew to 100 acres and firefighters were deployed to battle it. But by the next day, the Doe Fire had grown to 1,400 acres, and other fires in the area were also expanding across the relatively remote, mountainous terrain. By August 30, four of the largest fires—the Doe, Glade, Hull, and Tatham Fires—had merged. Eleven days later, this large conflagration joined with the Elkhorn and Hopkins Fires.

In all, the August Complex encompassed thirty-eight wildfires burning mostly in the Mendocino National Forest and a portion of the Shasta-Trinity National Forest. An estimated 446 structures were

Flames sweep toward homes as the August Complex Fire rages.
PHOTOGRAPH COURTESY OF CAL FIRE.

destroyed, but no civilian lives were lost. One firefighter working on the Tatham Fire was killed on August 31 when her truck tumbled off a steep road embankment into the fire and hit a tree. Another firefighter in the truck tried to pull her free as the windows shattered from the heat, but the flames were too intense. He managed to crawl back to the road, suffering extensive burns. Diana Jones, sixty-three, was a volunteer firefighter and emergency medical technician with the Cresson Fire Department near Fort Worth, Texas. She and her son, Ian Shelly, had traveled to California to fight fires for the season, as they had done for several years. "Diana was dedicated to trying to make people's lives a little bit better," said Cresson Fire Chief Ron Becker. "She was not any type of glory seeker. . . . She just wanted to make things better for people."

The August Complex was fully contained on November 12, 2020.

SOURCES

The Wildfires of 2017

2017 Incident Archive. CAL FIRE. https://www.fire.ca.gov/incidents/2017/.

Andone, Dakin. "The largest wildfire in California's modern history is finally out, more than 6 months after it started." CNN. June 2, 2018.

"California wildfire industry losses put at $13.2bn by Aon Benfield." Artemis. January 25, 2018.

"Encroaching Atlas Fire Spurs Evacuations for Parts of Fairfield." KPIX 5 CBS News. October 11, 2017.

No Rest for the Weary—2018 Wildfires

Associated Press. "California's Deadly Camp Fire Was the Costliest Natural Disaster of 2018, Insurer Says." *Time*. January 9, 2019.

Boxall, Bettina. "Redding was scorched by a wildfire so strong it created its own weather system." *Los Angeles Times*. July 28, 2018.

Espinoza, Martin, Nashelly Chavez, and Randi Rossman. "Firefighter who died battling Mendocino Complex fires mourned by Utah town." *The Press Democrat*. August 14, 2018.

"Fallen Utah firefighter Matthew Burchett remembered by family and comrades."
24/7 Help Group.

Fusek, Maggie. "Ranch Fire, the Largest Wildfire in CA History, Sparked by
Hammer." Patch. June 7, 2019.

Gabbert, Bill. "One year later, looking at the disastrous Northern California
wildfires." *Wildfire Today*. October 9, 2018.

Graff, Amy. "Evacuations ordered for east Chico as Camp Fire rages toward city
limits." SFGate. November 8, 2018.

Hernandez, Salvador. "Surrounded by California's Deadliest Wildfire, People
Jumped into a Lake and Creek to Survive." *BuzzFeed News*. November 14, 2018.

Johnson, Lizzie. "A Fire's Unfathomable Toll." *San Francisco Chronicle*.
April 26, 2019.

Krieger, Lisa M. "When survival means shelter." *San Jose Mercury-News*.
February 3, 2019.

Mack, Eric. "The Redding 'Fire Tornado' Is Something Scientists Once Thought
Was Too Unlikely to Worry About." *Forbes*. August 4, 2018.

Sabalow, Ryan, Ryan Lillis, Dale Kasler, Alexandra Yoon-Hendricks, and Phillip
Reese. "'This fire was outrunning us': Surviving the Camp Fire took bravery,
stamina, and luck." *Sacramento Bee*. November 25, 2018.

Seigel, Rachel. *California and Other Western Wildfires*. New York, NY: Crabtree
Publishing. 2019.

Serna, Joseph. "He feared being stung by wasps and accidentally started California's
largest fire." *Los Angeles Times*. June 8, 2019.

Serna, Joseph, Maria L. La Ganga, and Laura Newberry. "PG&E admits its
equipment likely sparked California's most destructive wildfire." *Los Angeles
Times*. February 28, 2019.

Simon, Caroline, Steve Kiggins, Mike Chapman, David Benda, and Alayna
Shulman. "'Destroyed': In Paradise, California, entire community of 27,000
was ordered to evacuate." *USA Today*. November 9, 2018.

Sullivan, Emily. "Camp Fire Missing-Persons List Grows to More Than 300
Names." National Public Radio. November 15, 2018.

Massive 2020 Wildfires

Benda, David. "Volunteer firefighter who died battling the California wildfires was a Texas mother on the front lines with son." *USA Today.* September 1, 2020.

Boxall, Bettina. "'Fires of hell': how dry lightning has sparked some of California's biggest infernos." *Los Angeles Times.* August 23, 2020.

Gabbert, Bill. "Firefighter killed on August Complex was assisting with backfire operation." *Wildfire Today.* November 5, 2020.

"Gov. Newsom Tours North Complex Fire Damage, Blames Climate Change." CBS News Sacramento. September 11, 2020.

KCRA staff. "LNU Lightning Complex: All evacuation orders lifted." KCRA 3 NBC News. September 11, 2020.

"Moisture from Tropical Storm Fausto fuels NorCal thunderstorms." *Los Angeles Times.* August 16, 2020.

Money, Luke and Joseph Serna. "Massive August fire now largest in California history, at 471,000 acres and counting." *Los Angeles Times.* September 10, 2020.

National Large Incident Year-to-Date Report. Northern California Area Coordination Center, National Interagency Fire Center. December 2, 2020.

Nicco, Mike, Drew Tuma, and Lisa Argen. "More lightning, thunderstorms hit Bay Area as heat wave continues." ABC 7 San Francisco. August 17, 2020.

North Complex Fire Incident Overview. InciWeb. National Wildfire Coordinating Group. Accessed December 2, 2020.

Romero, Ezra David. "As Bear Fire Tears Through Butte County, Berry Creek Residents Fear Their Town Is Gone." CapRadio. September 9, 2020.

SCU Lightning Complex Fire incident overview. CAL FIRE. October 1, 2020.

Stephens, Tim. "UC's Lick Observatory threatened by fire." UC Santa Cruz Newscenter. August 20, 2020.

Vainshtein, Annie. "LNU? SCU? CZU? How the Lightning Complex and other California fires get their names." *San Francisco Chronicle.* August 20, 2020.

INDEX

Page numbers in **bold** indicate illustrations. Page numbers in **bold** followed by **m** indicate maps.

ABOUT THE AUTHOR

PHYLLIS J. PERRY was born in Grass Valley, a small gold-mining town in northern California. She earned a BA in English Literature with a minor in History at the University of California, Berkeley. She taught in an elementary school of the Mt. Diablo Unified School District and earned her Master's in Education from San Francisco State University. During this time, she experienced the tremors of two earthquakes. Phyllis moved with her husband, David, and two daughters to Long Beach, where David taught at Long Beach State University and Phyllis taught part time at Golden West Junior College.

Phyllis and her family eventually moved to Boulder, Colorado, where her husband joined the faulty and she earned her doctorate in Education at the University of Colorado. Phyllis worked for twenty years in the Boulder Valley Schools as a teacher, building principal, and director of Talented & Gifted Education. Phyllis took early retirement to write full time. She is an award-winning author of fiction and nonfiction for both children and adults and is a member of the Colorado Authors' League and the Society of Children's Book Writers and Illustrators. Perry has written ninety-five books. In 2017, she received the Lifetime Achievement Award from the Colorado Authors' League.

Perry welcomes comments and can be reached through her website at www.phyllisjperry.com.

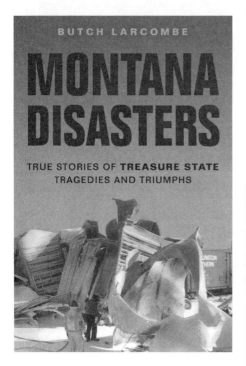
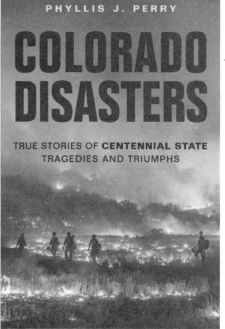